CROSSING
BORDERS

Wolfgang Pietrek

Crossing Borders
Wolfgang Pietrek

Design © 131 Design Ltd
www.131design.org
Text © Wolfgang Pietrek
www.wolfgangpietrek.com

ISBN 978-1-909660-65-6

Published 2016 by Tricorn Books
131 High Street, Old Portsmouth
PO1 2HW
www.tricornbooks.co.uk

Printed & bound in UK by CMP (uk) Limited

CROSSING BORDERS

To my wife ELAINE
and our sons
NICHOLAS and CHRISTOPHER
and their families

Contents

Introduction

Some people, often to the dismay and embarrassment of their partners, friends or hosts cannot resist arriving before an agreed time. Others sit in their cars or stand at the corner of the road, peering at their watches to make sure that their arrival is dead on time. They claim this to be an old-fashioned regal custom and a sign of good manners. Then there is the third category of individuals who quite enthusiastically embrace the concept that being on time is merely a human invention and ultimately a by-product of convenience.

Where does that leave me? Maybe I am in a category of my own. Whilst respecting the virtues of punctuality in daily activities, I take a decidedly more liberal attitude to the chronological passage of time. This, however, can easily lead to a laissez-fair attitude which lives in hope that a certain point in time is irrelevant and henceforth nothing needs to be done or - if left unattended - better things might turn up at a later stage.

It took me some time to realise that this attitude would have serious negative consequences for my ability to fulfil my long-held plan of recording my own personal passage through time.

Driven on by this overdue self-analysis I set about to record the highs and lows of my formative years covering the turbulent and traumatic episode of the last great European conflict. Apart from some anecdotal inclusions it is a summary of very personal experiences which not only made me witness the extremes of human brutality but which also let me see the outpourings of kindness and compassion by friends and strangers alike. It is the latter which has deeply enriched my life and it pains me that at this late stage I cannot express my personal thanks to all of them.

Along the road I had the great fortune of a caring and protective family and in particular of a mother who, in those post-war years of great hardship and distress, put her trust in me - which I am sure made me grow up before my time.

Even during the war good fortune was on my side when as an evacuee boy I ended up in the safe and caring environment of the Marlow family.

It is often said that we gather many acquaintances but very few friends. I had the great fortune of finding three trusted friends - Walter, Klaus and Gert - whose friendship I have treasured for many years now. Sadly Gert, my intrepid travel companion on our French Odyssey, passed away many years ago after having become a resident of Paris.

On that bleak April day in 1957 when I stepped onto that ferry in Calais, little did I know that this was to be another momentous milestone in my life as it started me off on a journey abounding with new borders and challenges.

NORTH SEA

BALTIC SEA

Warnemünde

Rostock

Lübek

Hamburg

Wismar

Lübz

Schwerin

Bremen

Hanover

Berlin

Münster

Magdeburg

Düsseldorf

Leipzig

Erfurt

Cologne

Eisenach

Bonn

Gotha

Dresden

Frankfurt

Nuremburg

Tübingen

Stuttgart

Freiburg

Munich

My Journey

Happy Days

My apologies for being late. When I looked up your postal address it struck me as being a rather rural area and therefore easy motoring, but what my Sat-Nav did not warn me about was the large number of roadworks and associated traffic lights I had to overcome first. However, here I am. My name is Joseph. You signed your e-mail to me with 'Wolfgang' so I presume you are either Austrian or German.

Well, Joseph, firstly welcome and no need to apologise for being a little late. On reflection I should have warned you of the roadworks in this area. Yes, my name is Wolfgang and I was born in Germany. You are not the first one to mention Austria as possibly my country of origin. The name Wolfgang almost automatically leads to an association with the celebrated composer Mozart and I have a suspicion that my parents, who were very fond of classical music, may have chosen it for me in the expectation that I also might develop some musical talents in later life. If there had been any slumbering talents, the war and the post-war years left little room for taking them to any heights.

It is my turn to apologise now, Joseph, because I have not even offered you any refreshment yet. I have a nice bottle of Alsace Riesling and some apple strudel, which I thought might sustain us during our journey through the past. And before I forget, please do not hesitate to stop or interrupt me at any time during my recollections.

The suggested refreshment will be most agreeable and I look forward with great anticipation to what you can tell me this afternoon. Judging by your age you must have been a young boy during the war years and probably a teenager in the equally traumatic post-war era. If I am not mistaken then, you must have been right in the midst of it all.

That is one way of describing it. So let me begin.

Excellent - I am all ears.

As you have already guessed, my arrival in this world was in the 1930s. I can now reveal to you that it was 1934.

It is a well-known phenomenon that with advancing years one's memory can play strange tricks. One can forget what one had for dinner the night before but long-term memories suddenly become sharper and vivid again. I am clearly going through this phase myself, which in turn prompted me to start piecing together again a multitude of past events. Some of the events have stayed very clear in my own memory, some are based on later hearsay and a large portion is based on what my parents and to a lesser extent also my grandparents passed on to me while they were still alive. It may sound strange to you, Joseph, but even to this date members of my own family are by and large unaware of my somewhat unorthodox childhood and teenage years.

My place of birth was the old Hanseatic town of Rostock which lies a few kilometres inland from the Baltic coast. The river Warnow, however, ensures easy access to the open sea at the picturesque old fishing village of Warnemünde. Whilst in the olden days fishing was the prime source of income for the villagers, it has over the years turned into an elegant seaside resort, on top of which it also became the ferry-port for the Berlin-to-Copenhagen train service. It was always a fascinating spectacle to watch the express train coaches being directly marshalled onto the large ferry boat for their voyage across the Baltic Sea to the Danish port of Gedser.

Nowadays you find the name of Warnemünde also on travel brochures as a port of call if you book yourself on one of the Baltic cruises. If you book a summer cruise you will see the white, long sandy beaches of Warnemünde filled with a large number of canopied beach chairs, many of them encircled by a low-level sand wall to mark the occupier's 'private domain'. Beach chairs could be hired for the whole summer season, which ensured that at any time one had access to one's own private retreat.

From my very early days my father always rented such a chair for the season and it was a real weekend treat for me and later on also for my younger brother to spend as much time as possible in our 'beach home'.

During my father's annual leave it was customary to visit

my paternal grandparents who lived in a faraway place called Leobschütz in Upper Silesia. This was always a full day's train journey during which, no doubt, my parents wanted me to sleep as much as possible.

In 1939 my parents abandoned the annual 'pilgrimage' to Upper Silesia and when we saw our mother preparing the picnic basket again we knew we would have some extra days at our much-loved 'beach home'.

This very same year had another big surprise in store for me: I was given a bicycle. It was in fact a girl's bicycle, which did not have a centre bar and was therefore much easier to mount. I still have a vivid memory of the occasion when my parents took me to the bicycle shop in Rostock's main shopping street, right behind the Kröpeliner Gate, one of the ancient gates providing entry into the inner city. The gift of a bicycle must have left a particularly strong impression on me, so much so that I even remember the name of that wonderful shop. It was called BLÜMEL. It took me only a few days to master the art of cycling and I soon gained sufficient confidence to accompany my parents on a bicycle ride to Warnemünde.

It was in fact after one of those bicycle rides to the beach that good fortune struck once again. Ever since I had been able to walk I had enjoyed scouring the wet sands just on the water's edge with my shrimp net in the hope of catching a few little crabs or shrimps. On this occasion I did not only find a few shrimps in my net but also a honey-coloured stone, which turned out to be a piece of amber.

My father intended to have it made into a piece of jewellery for my mother but with the menacing prospects of war and unrest it must have slipped down the list of priorities.

The other annual highlight was of course Christmas and all the preparations for it. My mother believed in baking the traditional stollen in September and the day before Christmas Eve my father used to bring in a large live carp that spent the night in the filled bath-tub. For the traditional carp soup on Christmas Eve the fish had to be really fresh. Our mother spent hours dressing the Christmas tree with strands of lametta, chocolate tree hangings and candles.

An added excitement was provided by our father. He was a devoted model railway enthusiast and every Christmas he filled our main sitting room with tracks and signals and shiny Maerklin engines and wagons.

All in all, these were very sheltered and happy childhood years, full of pleasant memories. In 1939 however, still being only five years old, I remained completely unaware of the racial and political turmoil which was already plaguing the whole nation and which would very shortly lead to a cataclysm of gigantic proportions for people of so many countries.

One can tell from your enthusiastic recapturing of your early childhood days that you started life in a very caring and protective environment and that life on the beaches and the wider outdoors played a big role in it. What did it actually mean in those days to live in a large urban conurbation? I would be interested to hear a little more about your birth place.

I am glad you brought me back to my initial theme, which was Rostock as my place of birth.

Strangely enough, when I ask people today if they know where and what Rostock is I very often get blank faces and on a few occasions I have even been told that it is a town in Russia. This may be an excusable mix-up with the truly Russian town of Rostov.

Rostock is now Mecklenburg's largest town and - as with so many parts of Central Europe - has been on a roller-coaster ride of different ownerships and jurisdiction during the last millennium.

After the Danes had driven out the resident slaves in the twelfth century, German merchants and craftsmen established a settlement on the banks of the river Warnow and from then on it kept growing into a thriving industrious and cultural centre on the shores of the Baltic sea. It is not surprising therefore that Rostock features among the founding members of the Hanseatic League, something that the present burghers of Rostock still recall with pride.

Its growing prosperity allowed the construction of formidable fortifications in the form of high walls and deep moats encircling the whole settlement. Access was provided by seven magnificent gate towers, four of which I believe are still standing today. In fact the number seven must have been revered by the Rostock burghers, because not only did they build seven gate towers but over the centuries Rostock also became the home of seven truly imposing churches, all of them within the walled township.

The fourteenth century was marked by a special event which attracted my very personal attention. Rostock bought the small fishing village of Warnemünde at the mouth of the river Warnow, thereby securing their full direct access to the Baltic Sea.

The profile of Rostock was further advanced when in 1419 it founded its own university, which laid claim to being the first university in Northern Europe.

During the next two centuries, however, Rostock suffered also the ups and downs of foreign occupations ranging from the Swedes to Wallenstein's troops to subdue the growing Protestant movement. And then the biggest disaster struck when in 1677 a fire destroyed large parts of the old town. With houses being mainly built of timber, town fires in those days must have been a constant danger as also demonstrated by the same calamity which had befallen London just a decade before.

However all this did not hold back the burghers of Rostock and they quickly rebuilt not only the old town but expanded its reach beyond the town walls with shipbuilding, adding a new dimension to its aspirations for the future.

In 1866 Mecklenburg finally became part of the kingdom of Prussia and Rostock found itself with new challenges.

Going back to my own geography lessons, I always had the impression that Mecklenburg was very much a rural and agricultural province with little or no industrial background.

You are absolutely right. Mecklenburg is a region of fertile soils, by and large very flat with a large number of picturesque lakes surrounded by woodlands and with small villages and market town dotted all over the country. The large country estates were a special feature; colloquially known as 'Rittergüter', they displayed their importance by often grandiose manor houses. Right into the late nineteenth and early twentieth century these estates were still run on a mild form of feudalism. At the same time however they were also the pioneers of many modern practices in agriculture.

With Rostock's view always directed towards the sea, it developed from a trading post into a sizeable industrial centre which seemed to have little in common with its agricultural hinterland.

The burghers of Rostock did not really like the idea of being looked upon as somewhat backward, a reputation which the rest of Mecklenburg province seemed to have acquired. It was even said that the German statesman Bismarck once insinuated that if the world were to perish tomorrow he would quickly travel to Mecklenburg, where everything happens 50 years later. In the event he could have encountered a few linguistic problems, because the low-German spoken in this part of Germany - and particularly in the countryside - can present genuine problems for outsiders.

Few large historical figures have emerged from this land but Rostock prides itself of being the birthplace of a man who, so some historians say, saved the British Empire. This was Fieldmarshal Blücher, who at the age of 72 and in command of the Prussian army, arrived just in time on 15 June 1815 to make sure the Duke of Wellington really won the battle of Waterloo. On reflection, the British owe quite a debt to Rostock.

Yes, I have also read several analytical reviews by eminent international historians who share your observation. I cannot imagine that in the turbulent years just ahead of you the British paid much attention to that vital support they had received in 1815, particularly with the memories of the horrific conflict of 1914-1918 still quite fresh in people's minds.

Yes, you are quite right. This new war was not going to be a conflict battled out in muddy trenches and with bayonet-raised charges over shell-holed fields filled with flesh-tearing rows of barbed wire. This time, apart from being fought out on land and sea, there was the additional horror of war from the air, claiming indiscriminately many lives, old and young. No doubt my reminiscences will bring me back to this topic later on.

As a Hanseatic town, Rostock had a long tradition of ship-building together with associated crafts and industries. It is to the credit of this enterprising community, always anxious to embrace new ideas and technologies, that by the middle of the nineteenth century it was here on the river Warnow that Germany's first iron-hulled and propeller-driven steamship was launched. Within a relatively short time, by the turn of the century, Rostock had developed into a sizeable ship-building centre for large cargo- and passenger-vessels: all the preconditions existed, therefore, for the future Rostock to become also an important Naval Base.

When, several years later - it was May 1945 - I rummaged through the partially destroyed and deserted Neptune shipyards I noticed the long and rather rusty looking narrow hulls of what looked like submarines, or U-Boats as they were more commonly known. Mountains of rubble, twisted metal cranes and fixtures as far as the eye could see. It was just another example of the ferocity of aerial bombardments. With a truckload of Russian soldiers appearing at the entrance gate to the yard, I decided on a hasty retreat.

Sorry, I have slipped into the future again.

The status of Rostock as a vibrant, enterprising commercial and industrial centre was further enhanced when in the 1920s the firms Heinkel and Arado built large production sites on the banks of the river Warnow between Rostock and Warnemünde. The very flat terrain provided the ideal conditions for building long runways for the aircraft produced at this site. The factories had their own railway station because virtually all the workers and employees resided in Rostock and commuted to and from the factories by train. In those days private motorised transport was still an expensive extravagance. The factory railway station became also quite a familiar stopping point for us whenever our family took the train to Warnemünde. The station had the unusual name of Marienehe and I never discovered why a somewhat religious name was chosen for what was basically the building block for a massive armaments establishment. Heinkel established an international reputation for their aircraft as reliable carriers for postal, cargo and passenger services. As you may recall, the treaty of Versailles did not allow German aircraft manufacturers to even experiment with anything of a militaristic nature. One can only assume that in the mid 1930s, with the new regime revving up the anti-Versailles rhetoric, the planning at Heinkel and Arado may well have included the drawings for future war planes. In 1939 the number of huge factory halls went up month by month.

As a newly qualified cyclist I became personally very aware of all the activities on the Heinkel site because the main road from Rostock to Warnemünde ran along the western periphery of the huge industrial complex. During the summer of 1939 I was allowed to accompany my parents on their bicycle rides to Warnemünde and it was on these occasions that even at my tender age, I noticed the ever-growing expansion of those factories. The distance from our home to the beaches was only around 10 kilometres but at my age and being a cycling novice I found these trips quite challenging. My younger brother Lothar did all this in the comfort of sitting in a cosy wicker chair on the back of my father's bicycle.

With the month of September almost upon you, did you ever get any impression from your parents' behaviour that any changes or upheavals lay ahead?

Not really, although I remember my parents talking more frequently about my paternal grandparents. Now, of course, I know that they were increasingly concerned about them as they were living quite close to the Polish-German border. The propaganda machine of the new regime had already primed the German population to believe that repeated Polish border transgressions could not be tolerated for much longer and that sooner or later a flare-up would occur.

And as you know, so it did finally on 1 September of that year.

War with Poland was bad enough, but the propaganda in the build-up to this confrontation had been so effective that the offensive into Poland found widespread support among the German population. What came as a shock to many, however, was that only two days later, Great Britain - after having given Germany an ultimatum to withdraw from Polish territory - declared war on Germany as a consequence of the existing British Treaty with Poland.

How history repeats itself! Only twenty-five years earlier Great Britain's treaty with Belgium had led to another gruesome slaughter between German and British armies.

When in later life I studied the events of September 1939 in more detail it always struck me as curious that only a fortnight later the then Soviet Union had invaded Poland from the East but London somehow 'forgot' to send a similar ultimatum to Moscow and confined its loyalty to Poland by declaring war only on Germany.

As one English historian once said to me: that is called 'Real Politic'.

With France now also declaring war on Germany the scene was set for yet another big European calamity.

The Clouds are Gathering

␣

*D*id the outbreak of war have a noticeable impact on your and
your family's life?

Not really. Social life continued as before. Theatres,
concert halls and cinemas enjoyed full attendances,
restaurants and coffee shops were as busy as ever. At
the same time the population was left in no doubt that
Germany was now at war. The Ministry of Propaganda
in Berlin were masters in using inflammatory language
to secure the unquestioned support of the majority of
the population. The 'honour of Germany' was at stake
and skilfully worded radio broadcasts and regularly
updated news-reels in the cinemas, glorifying the heroic
successes of the German armed forces, were powerful
tools to underpin popular support. I think someone in
Britain later on described the first few months of the
war as the 'phoney war'.

Preparations for Christmas were made as before and
I was reminded that early in the new year I would be
starting school. It was therefore no great surprise that on
Christmas Day I found a beautiful brown leather satchel
under the Christmas tree in our sitting room. On one

of our shopping trips into the town centre my mother took me past the school that I was going to attend and I realised that my future school days would involve quite a bit of walking.

In Germany it was customary to start primary school only at the age of six and as I never attended a pre-school kindergarten I had to rely on my parents to introduce me to the basics of writing and counting. For the latter we had a colourful abacus which I still think is a most effective device for young children to learn their numbers.

In early 1940, schools still taught the old German Gothic alphabet and just when I got to grips with that one, the Government suddenly decided that the Roman alphabet would become the official one. We had to start all over again.

I very much enjoyed my early school days and with time I even found that my walks to and from the school, situated just opposite the entrance to the main town cemetery, were not as challenging as I had originally feared.

It was really only in 1941 that we all began to feel a decided change in our lives.

Rostock as an important centre for the production of war planes and naval vessels led to some of the earliest British air raids on Germany and suddenly the horrors of death and destruction began also to register with us youngsters. The message really came home when, after having spent most of the preceding night in the cellar of our own home, on my way to school in the morning

I had to pass fire engines and rescue teams outside houses still smouldering. Bomb craters and unexploded bombs sometimes also led to major diversions on my way to school.

Quite often a putrid smell lingered in the air, a reminder of the hundreds of drums located in open spaces in and around the town. Whenever the early-warning sirens were sounded soldiers with gas masks released a kind of chemical fog from these drums, which then lay like a big cloud over large parts of the town and the surrounding area. With our home being quite close to one of the factories that supplied parts to the main shipyards we had the additional spectacle of seeing a few large balloons rising into the sky when the early alarms were sounded.

The most devastating and memorable impact of those early days of aerial bombardments was our sudden awareness that an empty desk in the classroom was no longer only the result of a pupil having a cold or some other health problem but that he may have been a victim of the previous night's air-raid.

How did youngsters of your age group react to the growing dangers and devastations surrounding you At the age of six-plus it is quite normal for children to begin to question the happenings around them.

They certainly do. In fact the questioning starts even earlier. In 1940, the year I started school, my daily walk to and from the school led me past the large army barracks in the Ulmenstrasse and I got quite used to seeing small groups of soldiers marching in and out of the compound. On one such occasion I saw a large column of soldiers emerging in different-looking uniforms and with caps adorned with a strange looking flower. When I later asked my father about the meaning of this flower I was told that it was called edelweiss and that it was the regimental markings for soldiers specialising in duties in mountainous terrain.

It was several weeks later, when the film in the cinema was preceded by the customary news-reel and I heard of the achievements of German Alpine troops in Norway, that I began to work out for myself that Rostock had been used as a transit camp. Somehow I felt quite privileged to have actually seen these soldiers.

With constant radio broadcasts and the always action-filled news-reels in the cinema, the extent and enormity of the ever-growing conflict began to register also with us youngsters, although we could not yet understand the real run-up and the complexities which led to so many confrontations in many parts of Europe and even Africa. The cruel reality of war was also brought home to me when, one day shortly before our school Christmas holiday, the young boy at the desk next to me reported that his father had been killed in France. It made me realise how lucky our family was with my father not being called up to serve in the armed forces.

Was your father exempted from military service?

My father was an electrical engineer with specialist knowledge in telecommunications and radio technology.

He was employed by the German Post Office, which in those days was not only responsible for the normal mail- and parcel services but which also maintained the whole national telephone network.

When war broke out, his specialist technical skills saved him from frontline duties but he was then called up to install and manage the early-warning system for air-raids in the Rostock area. While this allowed him to still live at home, there was many a night, following a sudden telephone call, when he would disappear. With my mother and brother Lothar, we spent many nights on our own in the cellar during air-raids.

In addition to his duties in Rostock, father was also called away to other locations in North Germany, including a short spell at the rocket production site in Penemünde, where apparently he was briefly involved in some research into remote control mechanisms. He never spoke about his work and I only heard this from him after the war.

Now let me go back to 1941, which saw not only the beginning of the gigantic conflict with the Soviet Union but which also produced one of the coldest winters Europe had seen for many years. My mother went to extra lengths to have me warmly wrapped up before sending me off to school. I even had to wear over-sized shoes to accommodate the extra thick socks.

One weekend, just before Christmas, the whole family took the train to Warnemünde to have a look at a rare spectacle. The Baltic Sea was completely frozen over and it was rumoured that one could actually have walked all the way across to Denmark.

I also remember the authorities pleading with the population to be generous with donations of all kinds of woollen garments, scarves, socks and gloves for the German troops in Russia. The temperatures there had also fallen to minus 40 degrees and many of the soldiers were still in their summer uniforms.

I assume from your recollections so far that your family home had escaped the ravages of the aerial bombardments.

Yes, we were very fortunate. During one night-raid, two incendiary bombs landed in the front garden of our home having missed the building by only a few metres. On impact they must have burst open releasing a cascade of a burning substance which not only melted the remnants of snow but destroyed the grass underneath too. All this I remember was accompanied by a hissing noise which we could clearly hear in our hideout in the cellar and a penetrating and cough-inducing smell. I learnt the next day that we had had the good fortune of having escaped two phosphor bombs, the likes of which had caused many fires in the older quarters of the town and had also led to more fatalities.

With the severity and frequency of air-raids ever increasing, the authorities started to evacuate schoolchildren and their teaching staff. It did therefore not come as a complete surprise to my parents, when they were informed that our whole class would jointly be evacuated at a date to be announced shortly. When the day came there were lots of wet faces, both young ones and older ones, and a flurry of pieces of advice on how to behave and in particular to remember to write home regularly. Our teacher and his wife, who were to be evacuated with us, were bombarded with questions on where the 'safer' location was - were we youngsters all going to board together in a large house or be distributed to individual families? Somehow our teacher seemed to know the answer to most questions and succeeded in calming many of the distraught parents.

I was accompanied to the train station by my mother and my younger brother Lothar. Our father was away somewhere. While mother also showed signs of a few tears she appeared very composed and maybe she saw the positive side of this heartbreaking event by thinking that at least one of her sons was no longer exposed to the horrors of the air-raids. My smart little leather suitcase was filled to capacity and I must admit that although I also felt quite apprehensive about leaving the familiar home surroundings, I almost began to look upon it as a kind of adventure.

Our class consisted of around 20 pupils. The train had a complete coach reserved for us and when we got into our allocated compartments we all tried to secure a place at the windows for the final farewell wave to our parents. Some of my fellow pupils were still crying when the train steamed out of the station and it was only after our teacher and his wife had toured all the compartments with reassuring words for the more distressed boys that a kind of fatalistic acceptance of the whole situation set in.

By the time you were on the train, did you have any idea as to where you were going?

Not exactly, but I had heard the name Lübz mentioned by our teacher when he was trying to answer the myriad questions posed by the parents. Geography or in our case 'Heimatkunde' had always been one of my favourite subjects at school and I remembered that Lübz was a small market town south of Rostock near the Lake District of Mecklenburg. And so it was.

Just before we arrived there our teacher came round to each compartment to inform us that the next stop would be our final destination and that we should get all our belongings together for a rapid disembarkation. We were then to meet outside the main gate of the station where arrangements for our onward transportation would be made. So Lübz was not our final destination after all.

After the teacher and his wife had made sure that the whole class had reassembled and that everybody had his baggage and belongings, we saw a rather shabby-looking bus pulling up in front of us. The elderly driver had two teenage helpers who put all our luggage on the fenced-in rooftop of the bus while our teacher told us to board the bus for our onward journey. I remember the bus engine labouring quite hard on an up-hill road out of Lübz, a road I was going to get to know quite well in the months to come.

As we were travelling along our teacher suddenly got up and turned round to address us. "Boys," he said, "the next village we come to will be your new home. It is called Broock and we shall be driving to the village schoolhouse where you will learn who your guardian parents are going to be. You will all have a day off to settle in and to get to know your new families but on the day after, classes will recommence in the school at 8.30 as usual."

Well, at least we knew now that our journey was approaching its end, but we were all filled with trepidation as to the new home and families who would now take on the role of our own parents back in Rostock.

It was only around 10 minutes later that we reached the village and the bus took a sharp right turn from the main road and drove down the central village road. It seemed to be the only road the village had, with small cottages neatly aligned on both sides. Halfway down the road was the village church and next to it finally the schoolhouse. There were quite a number of people in the school yard, mainly women of various ages. After disembarking from the bus we were told to line up in the yard and the some of the villagers stepped forward, taking a closer look at us.

It sounds like the setting for a modern slave auction.

I can see why you say that but it was in fact a practical procedure to give the villagers a chance of expressing their choices. After all, they were the ones who had volunteered to take an evacuee into their homes.

As the villagers filed past us, a woman stopped in front of me and asked for my name. She had a warm and friendly voice and I felt an instant liking for her.

"My name is Frau Malchow," she said, "and we live in a cottage just 200 metres from here."

After further questions from her about my own family and whether we had been bombed out in Rostock, I began to think that I had found my new home here in Broock. And so it was. I grabbed my suitcase, informed the teacher about my new host family and followed Frau Malchow to her home.

It was a pretty cottage with a large vegetable garden to the side. We did not enter the cottage through the front door but walked to the back where to my surprise I saw a long row of stables and barns and strange pieces of machinery. I had not expected all this behind a humble looking cottage.

We entered the cottage through a country-style kitchen with lots of shelves, a large oven and a massive wooden table dominating the space in the middle.

"Herr Malchow is working in the field today but he will be back before dusk," she said. "Come and I will show you your room. It is our son's room but he is in the army now."

I could hardly believe my luck. It was a light room

overlooking the village road, with a very comfortable-looking bed, a large oak wardrobe and a small table with two chairs. And I had all this to myself. When I took a quick glance out of the window I noticed that on the opposite side of the road was not another cottage but a long brick wall and a large black iron gate.

"Is that the entrance to some sort of castle?" I asked.

"No," said Frau Malchow. "That is one of our two Grossbauern we have in Broock and their large house is set back from the main road."

Was this one of the 'Rittergüter' you referred to earlier on?

No - as I found out later, the Grossbauer is merely a farmer with a significantly larger acreage of land than the smallholders to which the Malchows belonged.

To my own surprise I already began to feel at home here and after unpacking I remembered my mother's plea to write as soon as I had settled in, wherever that was. Before settling down to write I asked if the cottage had a telephone but was told that there were only four telephones in the whole village, one of which was owned by the 'Grossbauer' across the road. That meant letter writing from now on.

When I finally left my room Frau Malchow offered me a glass of milk and some bread with jam.

"Let me now show you round the outside," she said. "Meet our helper Louis and have a look at our animals."

For someone who had so far grown up in a big

cosmopolitan town, this was like a new world and I have to admit I began to like it more and more. The horse stable was empty but as we stepped outside into the yard again a cart with two horses came up the driveway. Frau Malchow waved to the man on the cart and I knew it was the moment to meet Herr Malchow. He was a stocky, cheerful-looking man and I felt immediately that he was a person with a kind heart.

"Let me put the horses away," he said "and then you must tell me all about your family and how the people in Rostock cope with the air-raids."

There was no sign of Louis but I was to learn a lot more about him in the days to come.

All in all it was a very satisfying new beginning and I must admit I did not feel very homesick. My new bed was truly comfortable and it was a nice feeling to know that one had an uninterrupted night's sleep ahead with no likelihood of being wakened by the piercing sound of the early-warning sirens. There was just the odd distant muffled sound of cows mooing, which I found rather soothing.

I get the impression that having landed with this family you felt like you'd won the lottery.

That is one way of describing it.

Our first school day was particularly exciting as it gave us all the opportunity to exchange news about our new host families, how we had been received, what our accommodation was like and what kind of food was being served. Most of my fellow pupils expressed great satisfaction with their new hosts, some were not quite sure yet and I of course was very enthusiastic.

It was also the first opportunity to meet the young boys and girls from the village, whose classroom was next to ours. I was surprised there were so few of them but then Broock was really only a small village and the older children, I heard, were bused off to a school in Lübz every morning.

It must have been the very first week at school when on my way back to the cottage I was overtaken by a gentleman holding a young girl by her hand. I had seen her before in the school yard and when passing me they greeted me and asked me what my name was and where I lived. When I told them that I was with the Malchow family the gentleman said that they lived just across the road. I guessed then that he must be the 'Grossbauer'.

"Come over and see us tomorrow afternoon," said the gentleman. "It's my wife's birthday and there could be a piece of cake waiting for you."

I was quite taken aback by such spontaneous friendliness. I did not hesitate to say yes.

"Good. See you then tomorrow at 4 o'clock and this young lady here, by the way, is called Liese."

When I reported to Frau Malchow my encounter with the 'Grossbauer' and the invitation she said that I was rather privileged because the 'Grossbauer' had a reputation of being very selective about who he invited to his house.

That same afternoon I finally also got an opportunity to talk to Louis, the farm hand, who turned out to be a French prisoner of war. He was a man of about thirty years of age and spoke almost fluent German, albeit with a strange accent. He told me that he came from a place called Mülhausen, a town in Alsace right on the border with Germany.

In the weeks and months to come Louis became a great tutor to me on how to deal with the animals, harness up the two horses, milk cows without having the bucket kicked over by the animal, collect eggs from the henhouse beside the barn, clean out the stables and many other jobs which occur on a farm. One of my favourite tasks before going to school was to lead the Malchow's small herd of sheep out of the barn onto the village main road where they then joined dozens of other sheep who, led by a shepherd, made their way to the common grazing grounds outside the village. It always amazed me how orderly this daily migration was and how on their return early in the evening the Malchow sheep knew exactly where to peel off from the rest of the main herd and return to their own enclosure in the barn.

It was around the same time every early evening that Louis said goodbye to us. He then walked down to the end of the village, normally together with half a dozen other young men. Nothing was ever said about this strange daily procedure and being inquisitive by nature I followed this group of young men one evening, to see them all boarding a small bus in a side road. On my return I could not resist asking my host for some explanation and I then learnt that all those young men were prisoners of war and whilst working as farm hands during the day they had to return to a nearby camp every evening.

It sounds a rather cosy arrangement for prisoners of war and almost an open invitation to escape, particularly when like Louis, they spoke good German.

During all my time in Broock none of the prisoners ever made an attempt to escape. Their life in Broock was comfortable, their home land occupied and the trauma of previous fighting may have discouraged them from trying to take up arms again. Louis never talked about his own war experience and how he became a prisoner.

My visit to the 'Grossbauer' turned out to be the beginning of a useful and interesting relationship. Compared with the stables and barn of my host family everything here was on a much larger scale. The empty cowshed looked large enough for a whole herd of cows and a row of horseboxes indicated that this farm was not short of horsepower. I also noticed a glossy black carriage, similar to one I had once seen in a picture book.

When the 'Grossbauer' asked me if I would like to come back the following Sunday I did not hesitate a second to say 'yes'. Another very important discovery was that there was a telephone in the hallway, which the 'Grossbauer' indicated was available to me if I needed it.

To make the next visit even more appealing I was told

that I could then exercise one of their horses in the inner farmyard.

Good fortune really seemed to be with me and my weekly letter to my parents was a reflection of all this.

It must have been towards the end of April when the radio mentioned aerial activity in the Rostock region and the downing of several enemy aircraft. When I phoned my mother I could tell immediately that she was very shaken as she tried to explain that - while we were speaking - huge fires were apparently still raging through the lower parts of the town and that in the town centre several churches and many houses had been completely destroyed. Fortunately our home and indeed the district where we lived had escaped this tragedy. Little did we all know at this stage that in the following three nights Rostock would suffer further air-raids with devastating results and many fatalities. As I found out later, the Christus Church, where I had been baptised, also suffered a hit and lost its steeple. It was years later that I learnt that the raiders had adopted a new system of bombing, described as 'carpet bombing'.

Several days later I received a letter from my parents describing in much more detail the tragic events of those four nights and mentioning also that two friends of our family had perished. My parents also expressed the fear that Rostock being an important centre of armament production with our shipyards and the huge Heinkel factories may have to face more raids in the future.

My hosts were really shocked when they heard what the people of Rostock had to go through when here in Broock life was so peaceful.

It was many years later that I learnt that the devastation caused to my home town led to a specifically targeted retaliatory raid by the Luftwaffe on the English town of Bath, best known for its Roman origin but unlike Rostock of little military importance

With the summer holiday upon us my knowledge of farming life was extended even further since Herr Malchow and also Louis considered me strong enough to help actively with the harvesting of the cereal crops. Fortunately the fields were scattered over a wide area around the village and I was allowed to take the reins of Hans and Moll to drive the cart and equipment from field to field. My first real challenge came when Herr Malchow showed me how to hold a scythe and how to swing it for a clean cut of the stalks just above the ground. The tool looked a really lethal weapon but after some words of encouragement from Louis I quickly developed a good swing and quite enjoyed seeing the stalks fall into neat layers.

Louis and I now had to cut a strip of wheat at the edge of the field, wide enough to allow Herr Malchow to bring Hans and Moll onto the field, pulling a large mechanised cutting device. With this machine the rest of the crop was cut down in no time. Then however came the more demanding task of gathering the stalks in to bundles which then were built up into small stacks.

And all this in soaring temperatures. At the end of each day I felt quite proud to have made a real contribution to the harvesting process.

Going by your enthusiastic recollections so far you have clearly taken to the rural life like a duck to water.

Yes, you may well say that. It got even better when I was asked to take Hans and Moll for re-shoeing to the village blacksmith and also drive the cart with the dried crops all the way from the fields to the big threshing machine in the village. I was fascinated to watch this huge noisy machine discharging at the rear large bales of tightly strapped straw and spewing out the corn seeds into a big metal container at the other end.

The autumn season brought new challenges. After harvesting the sugar beet in rather inclement weather conditions, my host asked me to accompany him with the drilling in of the wheat and barley seeds for the next season's crop. My skills in milking cows got better week by week and to add to the diversity of farm life, a man had arrived a couple of weeks earlier to shear the small herd of sheep.

There were also sad moments when one day a truck turned up and took away one of the pigs.

One Sunday, just before Christmas, the 'Grossbauer' sent a farmhand across the road with a note asking me if I would like to accompany them on a trip to Lübz the following day. Herr and Frau Malchow gave their instant approval. When on the next day I entered the

'Grossbauer's' inner yard, the elegant black carriage with two beautifully harnessed horses stood at the entrance to the house. The whole family appeared with blankets over their arms and even an extra one for me. Liese and her mother seated themselves in the back row of the carriage and the 'Grossbauer' and myself settled down upfront.

When driving through the village I was really hoping that some of my fellow pupils or even the teacher could see me in all this splendour.

Outside the village I was asked to take over the reins. It was a thrilling day out. The 'Grossbauer' and his family were obviously well known in Lübz as many people greeted them. After some shopping and a visit to the brewery we returned to Broock, with me driving the carriage back all the way. A memorable day out.

Were you not all anxious to get back to your families for Christmas?

Yes, we were all keen to get back home for the festive season but the authorities had made no arrangements for such a return and we were told that we would spend Christmas with our host families.

Once again good fortune was on my side. I could hardly believe my eyes when a small red car pulled up outside the cottage and my father stepped out of it.

He was on an inspection tour of telephone stations and radio transmitters which had taken him to Plau, a lakeside village not far from Broock.

This was my father's first opportunity to meet my hosts and I also introduced him to the 'Grossbauer' opposite. Everybody was keen to hear first-hand how Rostock had suffered during the April raids and how people were coping.

My Christmas present was a small Meccano set, plus a scarf my mother had knitted for me. He also had a parcel for my hosts but I never discovered what was in it. After having been shown round the cottage, the stables and the barn, my father had to bid farewell as he said he had to get to the town of Güstrow that evening and the road conditions looked rather difficult. My hosts also gave him a parcel, presumably filled with some of the tasty items from their big larder. Maybe in order to console me, my father mentioned just before departing that this Christmas he had not set up the model railway in the sitting room and that my brother Lothar would have other toys to keep him happy.

Christmas at the cottage was different from what I was used to at home. Firstly there was no Christmas tree - just a few candles - and no carp in the bath tub for the traditional Christmas Eve fish soup.

Our teacher had summoned us all to a Christmas service in the village church which was also attended by many of the villagers, including the 'Grossbauer' and his family. My hosts, however, did not attend. In the congregation I noticed a few women dressed completely in black and a man with a black ribbon round his jacket sleeve. As the radio kept reminding us, we were at war.

With the onset of the new year, life in the village carried on in its customary fashion. Now I was in my final year of primary schooling the curriculum had become more diverse and also more demanding. That, however, did not stop me from giving a helping hand on the farm wherever I could: feeding the animals, cleaning stables and also helping Louis in the vegetable garden. Then the weekly letter to my parents. The 'Grossbauer' had not forgotten me either and asked me over from time to time to exercise his horses in the yard or even in the larger field at the back of his farm.

My hosts, always worried about the fate of their son, were delighted to receive a letter from him saying that he had been transferred to a non-combat role although he could not say where he was.

Letters from my mother also inferred that air-raids were now very infrequent - a great relief after the traumatic April week the previous year - and that there was talk about bringing evacuee children back home to Rostock. With that possibility in mind, she wrote, we have already provisionally booked a place for you at the Gymnasium.

I have to admit that at that moment I was not even sure if I wanted to rush back to Rostock so quickly.

Herr Malchow took me on a tour of the fields one day to let me see for myself how our drilling effort the previous autumn had resulted in healthy green fields, promising another good harvest. It gave me quite a feeling of satisfaction to know that in a minor way I had made a contribution to the different tasks on the farm and that my host recognised this.

At the end of April, I think it was during the Easter week, the village was hit by a tragic accident, when a large barn behind one of the cottages went up in flames. The town fire brigade from Lübz arrived remarkably quickly and although the barn could not be saved, the firemen at least stopped the fire from spreading to adjacent buildings. Thankfully the farmer managed also to save all his animals who had been stabled in the barn.

At the end of June we were finally told that we were all going back to Rostock and to ready ourselves for departure in the first week of July. I felt quite sad going round the village to say goodbye to some of the villagers I had got to know well - the blacksmith and above all the 'Grossbauer' and his family. All of them hoped that one day I would come back for a visit.

When the day of departure came I also did a farewell round of the stables, stroked Hans and Moll for the last time and then went to the schoolyard - accompanied by my hosts and Louis - where the bus was waiting to take us back to the railway station in Lübz. It was an emotional goodbye. Apart from my own suitcase I also had a large parcel given to me by Frau Malchow filled with a variety of tasty farm produce.

Did all your fellow pupils become as attached to the village and the rural life as obviously you did?

Most of us did, but there were also a few who never

gave up being homesick and also some where life with the host family was not as warm and friendly as I had experienced.

The train journey home took us also through Güstrow, the place my father had mentioned when he surprised me with his pre-Christmas visit.

The platform in Rostock was crowded with parents and grandparents giving their returning children a noisy welcome. My mother had turned up with Lothar but my father was missing. On our tram journey back to our home we passed through the centre of the town and I got my first impression of the devastation caused by the traumatic raids during April of the previous year.

It was good to be home again and also to play the part of Big Brother but for quite some time my mind wandered back to the life on the farm, the animals, the comfortable room I had all to myself and the friendliness of my host family. One compensation was that I could now visit Warnemünde again, although the old canopied beach chairs were no longer there.

Only a week or so after my return to Rostock the authorities arranged a holiday trip for boys of my age-group to a youth camp in the Harz mountains. It only dawned on me years later that we were the age-group which was approaching the age of 10 and that this was probably a camp to give us a taste of future activities as members of the Jungvolk, the junior version of the Hitler Youth. When we heard of our final destination and - above all - that we were to travel via the great city of Hamburg, all us youngsters were very excited.

Did you all expect to get a day off in Hamburg for sightseeing?

I was not sure what to expect and in any case the events which unfolded left us no choices. It was a Saturday in July 1943 when our train set off west towards Lübeck and then on to Hamburg. The city had already suffered some earlier air-raids causing fires in various parts of this great city but fire brigades were said to have kept these well under control. With the onset of darkness our train pulled into the large Hamburg Central Station. We were told to disembark with our baggage and to follow our Group Leader, who led us to an enormous concrete bomb shelter very near the station. Nothing of this size existed in Rostock.

There were lots of benches and even bunk beds and a few trolleys came along to provide us with hot soup. It all looked very organised.

It was not long after this that we heard the now familiar sound of the air-raid sirens and an hour or so later the bombardment became so intense that one could feel vibrations even in this huge block of concrete. I thought of my aunt Lotte and uncle Peter who lived in Hamburg. Would they survive this inferno?

As we emerged from the shelter in the morning we were hit by hot air with debris lying everywhere, nearby buildings still burning and a general atmosphere for which the word 'inferno' is very fitting.

Strangely enough the main track and the railway station itself had survived the raid and with thick smoke still hanging over the area round the station we managed to re-board our train, which then quickly proceeded southwards to the Harz mountains. Little did we know at that moment that the last night was merely the beginning of more devastating air-raids that would in the end destroy most of this beautiful old Hanseatic town.

On the train the Group Leader informed us that he had been able to telephone his office in Rostock, asking them to pass messages to all the anxious parents that their children had survived the raid on Hamburg unharmed.

I do not remember the name of the railway station where we finally disembarked. Buses were waiting to take us to the holiday camp, which seemed to be located in the middle of a huge forest. The wooden huts provided very comfortable accommodation with individual beds and spacious shower rooms.

A good-size sports field allowed us to play our favourite game of handball but also the occasional football match. During the regular excursions into the forest our Group Leader taught us about edible and poisonous mushrooms, explained the different types of trees and also the birds and animals we encountered. I did not let on that my father had taught me most of those things already during our Sunday trips in the forests around Rostock.

The food was plentiful and varied but not anywhere near the standard which my mother or Frau Malchow had provided. Evenings were taken up with board games and often supplemented with narrow-gauge films, predominantly highlighting the achievements of our Regime.

I made a few new friends, two of whom later became fellow pupils at the Rostock Gymnasium. The two weeks in the camp really passed more quickly than I had anticipated.

Our return journey to Rostock was routed via Magdeburg and uneventful compared with the outward journey only a fortnight earlier.

I learnt years later that after the devastating air-raids the authorities had in fact forbidden all civilian traffic into Hamburg to stop people from being psychologically affected by the sight of such devastation.

After my return to Rostock my mother informed me that our Hamburg relations had thankfully survived the raids but that their home and the whole surrounding area had been destroyed.

I read somewhere myself that, after Dresden, Hamburg was the most affected city with most of the huge number of fatalities caused by fire storms.

Yes, I believe that was the case. It was the massive use of incendiary bombs containing phosphor that so dramatically changed the conduct of air warfare, as it was clearly designed to destroy the resolve of the civilian population.

Life back in Rostock almost assumed an air of normality. I finished my last term at the old primary school and used some of my spare time to visit the parts of the town which had suffered so badly the previous year.

On my way to school I always had to pass very near the Christus Church, where I had been baptised in March 1934. The church had not only lost its steeple during the April air-raid but had also suffered much damage inside. Surprisingly, the priest's house next to the church had not been damaged at all. On my exploratory wanderings through Rostock I discovered that of the seven magnificent places of worship within the walled town, four had been completely destroyed.

It must have been around this time that my own religious orientation became more focussed. Since my father's family had a strong Catholic background, my baptism into the Catholic Christus Church had been a foregone conclusion. My mother, however, came from a Lutheran family and whenever the opportunity existed - particularly with my father's often prolonged absence - she took me along to the Lutheran St Johannis Church. This in a way suited me quite well because I was already very friendly with the Pastor's son who had also been an evacuee to Broock.

Years later, in April 1950, my friend's father, Pastor Gallay, confirmed me into the Lutheran Church and my own father accepted it later without any protest.

Christmas approached very rapidly and I was wondering

if father would set up the model railway again. Shortly before Christmas Eve the big box with the railway station, tracks, signalling pieces and the engines and coaches appeared in the sitting room and my father suggested that since I was now nearly 10 years old, I and my brother Lothar should try to set the circuit up ourselves and that he would then attend to the electrical connections. We readily accepted this challenge. My mother busied herself with dressing the Christmas tree with plenty of lametta and I really felt it was Christmas like in years gone by. One thing, however, was missing. My parents did not succeed in obtaining a carp for our traditional fish soup.

With bombing raids having virtually ceased during this period, one could almost have thought it was peacetime again had it not been for the radio, which reminded us daily of military successes but more and more also of strategic corrections of front lines, particularly in the Soviet Union. I did not understand at the time that this really meant serious military setbacks.

Did your parents ever comment about the events unfolding on the eastern front?

I am sure my parents discussed the increasingly precarious state of the war amongst themselves but never in our presence.

With my tenth birthday approaching I was now not only a pupil of the Gymnasium at the Rosengarten but readying myself also to becoming a member of the Jungvolk. I do not remember if it applied to young girls too, but all boys were automatically enrolled into the Jungvolk when reaching the age of ten. At the enrolment centre I was kitted out with my uniform plus a black belt and shoulder strap and a strange-looking knot formed by strands of leather, through which I was to feed my black necktie. Together with my knee-length grey socks and black shoes I thought that overall it was a smart outfit that gave me the feeling of being much more grown up.

Life at the new school became decidedly more demanding than what I had experienced so far. The first challenging new addition to the curriculum was Latin followed not much later by ancient Greek with an unfamiliar new alphabet. Unfortunately, being located very close to the town centre, we had no playing fields and only a small yard behind the school to serve as an exercise yard.

It must have been around May when we were informed that the whole school, including all the teaching staff, would be evacuated from Rostock. This was now my second evacuation within two years. This time our destination was the country town of Malchin, located in a region which was known as the Switzerland of Mecklenburg.

Once again I packed my leather suitcase, now even heavier with extra school books, and then there was another emotional farewell at the Rostock railway station. This time, with so many pupils of various ages and also the teaching staff plus their families, we must have filled a whole train.

Our train passed through Güstrow again as it had done on my previous evacuation, but then headed east.

At the Malchin Station we were received by a row of buses, but next to them were also two horse-drawn carts, onto which we were asked to load all our baggage.

Our final destination was only a few kilometres outside Malchin and was quite awe-inspiring. It was a small village with just one row of little houses and a few very large barns behind them. At the end of the village road was a large ornate iron gate, the entrance to a tree-lined driveway that led to a large imposing building.

I had heard about the magnificent residences owned by some of the aristocratic estate owners. This was obviously one of them and must have been requisitioned by the authorities to become our new home. The magnificent entrance hall gave an immediate impression of the splendour which must have existed here in the past.

There were long corridors with many doors on both sides and - as we soon discovered - most of the rooms had been converted to dormitories with bunk beds and rows of wardrobes and shelves. The rooms had six bunk beds for the Jungvolk boys and one normal bed for the room captain, who was always a senior boy and already a member of the Hitler Youth. Then there was one large wing of the building set aside for the teachers and their families and on the ground floor, on both sides of the magnificent entrance hall, were several larger rooms which were to become our classrooms. At the back, towards the gardens, was another big hall which was partially a kitchen but also our canteen.

After a short settling-in period, life began to acquire a slightly military style.

Every morning, whatever the weather conditions, we had to assemble on the large lawn at the back of the house and stand in orderly lines for the hoisting of the flag, followed by a senior pupil reading out the activity programme for the day. This was occasionally supplemented with news items from the war fronts.

After breakfast, school classes took up the morning.

Did you at this stage already feel that you are being groomed to become an unquestioning believer in the regime's ideology?

Sometimes thoughts of that kind passed through my mind, but at the same time I felt secure and well looked after and the non-curricular activities were very exciting. Twice a week this included target shooting with powerful air rifles and then there were outings into the neighbouring fields and forests to learn about map-reading and orienteering. Whenever possible I avoided getting too involved in boxing, wrestling and other physically demanding exercises.

In the classroom our teachers maintained a strict regime. We all liked our Latin teacher who we called Gandhi because he once told us that his parents had lived in India and that he was born out there. The least-liked teacher was our biology teacher who used the cane for the slightest misdemeanour. He was so disliked that a small group of us decided to take our revenge on him. He was a middle-aged bachelor with a physical impediment. He had a wooden leg which we had discovered he always left at his bedroom door before retiring. As it was the rule throughout the building that no doors were ever locked, two of my fellow pupils and myself hatched a plan to steal the wooden leg one night, and - if successful - to leave an anonymous note in the entrance hall the following afternoon to disclose the whereabouts of the leg.

We all knew that our room captain was a very sound sleeper, which would enable us to sneak out of our room late at night to carry out this dangerous undertaking. Our raid on the teacher's room went off without a hitch and the leg was hidden in an antique cupboard in the entrance hall. We safely returned to our bunk beds with the room captain still sound asleep.

After the traditional morning assembly and flag-hoisting the Headmaster stepped in front of us all for a special announcement. The three of us had a good idea what this announcement was going to be about.

"I expect the perpetrator or perpetrators of this disgraceful act to step forward to firstly apologise for their action," he said. "For those who do not know, Mr Ebert's leg was removed from his room last night. Secondly I want to hear right now where the leg is hidden."

The three of us had promised each other that we would stick together come what may and consequently no-one stepped forward to admit guilt or disclose the whereabouts of the leg. We must have tried very hard to look as innocent as possible. Strangely enough there was quite a bit of subdued giggling going on amongst the assembled pupils and teachers when they heard the Headmaster's address. The biology teacher was not only disliked by many pupils but also seemed to have few friends amongst the teaching staff. As planned we left a note that afternoon on a table in the entrance hall, disclosing the hiding place and the matter was never raised again.

I would call this a narrow escape and presumably it provided a topic for conversation and speculation for many days afterwards.

It certainly did. Yet we were never suspected as we were regarded as far too young to plan and execute such a daring raid.

As the months went by most of our daily life was confined to the Manor House and the surrounding fields and woods. Outside the wrought iron gate, behind two of the village cottages, were some large barns and stables. Although this part of the estate was not officially off-limits we were encouraged not to stray beyond the gates. This of course only increased our curiosity.

One afternoon, it must have been late October, one of my room mates and myself sneaked out of the estate grounds to take a closer look at the barns and stables.

As we approached we heard voices. We opened a small side door into the barn and were truly amazed by what we saw. There were dozens of rather doleful-looking people of all ages, surrounded by bags, suitcases and a variety of belongings and further back in the barn were several carts and some sad-looking horses. A rather well-built woman stepped forward to ask us if we lived in the village. We told her that we were in fact evacuees from Rostock and that our whole school was now residing in the nearby Manor House. More of these people formed a group around us as they seemed eager to tell us their tragic story. They were all people from the Memel Land and the far corners of Eastern Prussia who had fled from the advancing Soviet forces. It was quite difficult for us to fully understand what we had just heard because none of this ever came to light in the daily news or announcements at the morning assemblies.

We had overheard some of the senior pupils talking about the escalating conflict in France but were not aware of enemy armies actually penetrating into the German homeland, as was now obviously happening in the East. My friend and I agreed that it would be best not to share our experience with any of the other pupils.

School curricula remained by and large non-political. Our modern history books however, reflecting the views of the Hitler regime, gave a very comprehensive coverage of the 1914-1918 war, and emphasised the injustices of the 1919 Versailles treaty. Some of this, as I learnt years later, found considerable resonance with the general public, including my parents. It was widely seen as an act of brutal vengefulness after what was in reality an armistice in November 1918 with no foreign armies on German soil.

The devastating financial burden of reparations to be paid to the former enemy nations, the occupation of the Saarland by France, and other punitive measures clearly led to the ensuing period of extreme hardship and hyper-inflation.

These grievances were widely shared throughout the nation and not only by people who in the 1930s had so enthusiastically supported the rise of Hitler. Looking back with adult eyes, I am even more of the opinion that any disgruntled and disillusioned nation or society can be swayed in their actions and behaviour by someone with demagogic powers. If the Germans had not secretly shipped Lenin from Switzerland to Russia in 1917 to mobilise an angry and disillusioned population against their rulers, a year later he could probably have achieved the same in Germany and more quickly than Hitler ever did. Just imagine, Lenin's mausoleum could have been at the Brandenburg Gate instead of Red Square.

Sorry about this sudden excursion into the past, but modern history has always been a favourite topic for me.

I am delighted you broached this subject because it is something I have been thinking about from time to time without ever really coming to any finite conclusion. But then, history is not a science. Two and two do not always make four. I regard it more as a record book of events, good and bad, from which we could learn to avoid future mistakes. But do we?

I am sure you know the answer yourself.

Now let me come back to life at the Manor House. As the most recent recruits to the Jungvolk we were particularly targeted with intense indoctrination of the regime's ideology. This was done by a number of the most senior pupils who were already fanatical supporters of the regime and always turned up in their Hitler Youth uniform, but also by two teachers who were obviously members of the NSDAP, the ruling Nazi Party. As later events demonstrated, the mind-manipulation of young boys can have quite traumatic results.

It was only six months later, in April 1945, that boys from my age group volunteered to carry soup and provisions and possibly even ammunition to forward military positions on the eastern perimeter of Rostock, where - in a futile attempt - some units of Volkssturm assisted by Hitler Youth boys were ordered to halt the advancing Russian army.

As I learnt later, all they achieved was to blow up a bridge over the river Warnow and delay the advance of the Russian troops by a few hours. A short but intense artillery barrage merely added to the already heavy destruction of the eastern part of the town. Casualties amongst the hapless defenders were high and those being taken prisoner faced the frightening prospect of spending years in Russian labour camps. It must have been a particularly gruesome realisation for the captured Hitler Youth youngsters, who were only a few years older than me.

All this was still to happen as now we were still all at the Manor House anxiously waiting for the return journey to Rostock for the Christmas holiday. We were told to take all our belongings with us, which indicated that after Christmas we might not be returning to Malchin and the Manor.

With the onset of 1945 the increasingly precarious military situation could no longer be glossed over by the propaganda machine of the regime. The ever-increasing stream of refugees from the East forced the authorities to reallocate transport and housing for the resettlement of the refugees. Our return to Malchin was officially cancelled, which did not really come as a surprise. We resumed our schooling at the Gymnasium at the Rosengarten in Rostock, in fact in the very same classroom as before.

Strange as it may sound, in all this mayhem and destruction around us, cultural and artistic events were not completely abandoned. In early January our school was invited to send two pupils with good treble voices to sing as guest choristers with the Thomaner boys' choir at the St Thomas Church in Leipzig., the church in which no lesser person than Johann Sebastian Bach was once the organist and choir master. A few boys were asked to assemble in the school's music room for tests and a rehearsal and I turned out to be one of the chosen two. When I got home that day my parents could hardly believe it. My father was particularly pleased about this. He himself was an enthusiastic amateur pianist and had occasionally expressed his disappointment that the war situation and my prolonged evacuations had not allowed me to progress with my piano lessons. His son being asked to go to Leipzig was something he really looked upon as a musical accolade for the family. Also my mother could hardly cover her excitement that I had been chosen for such a privileged assignment.

Then calamity struck and we were quickly reminded that we were still at war.

The day before we were due to travel, our music teacher - who would have accompanied us - informed us that heavy air bombardments in and around Leipzig had destroyed rail access from the north and that the trip had to be cancelled. Fortunately the St Thomas Church remained unharmed. It was 38 years later, on a business trip to Leipzig, that I finally managed to visit the Church and see the choir stalls where I would and should have sung as a young boy. It was quite a moving moment.

In late February my father was posted away again and left with an especially heavy heart since we were about to have another addition to the family. In March my baby brother Dietmar arrived and thankfully my mother was only away in hospital for two days, during which a lady family friend from Warnemünde looked after us two boys. When my father phoned to find out if mother and baby were alright, he did not seem to be surprised that it was yet another boy.

He told us later that for three generations the first-born

son in the family always had had male siblings and since he was a first-born, he was sure it would be another boy. Strangely enough that genetic tradition seems to have been passed on to me as well.

With the ever-growing realisation of unavoidable defeat, did the people by and large maintain their composure or was fear already setting in about the harsh treatment most likely to be handed out by the enemy powers?

Naturally there was mounting nervousness among the people, particularly with regard to the Soviet Union. Ever since 1941 the regime had promoted the image of the 'brutal Bolshevic' and reports from the refugees from the eastern provinces of Germany sometimes added to this perception.

Rumours of the most bizarre nature were circulating throughout the community.

One of them was that Germany still had Super Weapons, or Wunderwaffen, as they were officially referred to, both at sea and in the air to be used at any moment. By mid-April this reached a new climax with a story making the rounds that the new American President Truman was an ardent anti-communist and that he would side with the remaining German army to halt the advance of the Russian forces into western Europe.

Little did we know about the post-war plans already agreed upon in Yalta.

Finally, after that short artillery barrage on the eastern part of the town, Russian troops entered the outskirts of

Rostock on 1 May 1945. Unbeknown to all of us, Hitler had taken his own life only two days earlier.

In those final days of the war there were no defensive military positions on the territory to the west of Rostock and many civilians used the relative calm in that region to flee westwards.

One very strange event is specially engraved in my memory. It was 2 May when suddenly a lone German soldier in full uniform, armed with a light machine gun and with strings of ammunition over his shoulder, came down our road and went into the front garden of the house next door. As civilians we knew that the eastern parts of the town were already in the hands of the Russians, but somehow this soldier - who had obviously been separated from his Unit - was completely unaware of the true situation. Our neighbour quickly informed the German soldiers of what we knew and without having to use much persuasion, the machine gun, ammunition and helmet were taken behind the house to the back garden, where with the help of the soldier a hole was dug quickly to bury the unwanted equipment for good.

Thereafter my mother sprang into action. To save the lone soldier from being taken prisoner we had to turn him into a civilian and also burn his uniform and get rid of his heavy boots. My mother must have quickly sized up the young soldier's physique and seemed to know where to find something suitable for him. He was certainly too tall to fit into any suit of our father's. As it happened our immediate neighbour in our apartment block had been a senior policeman. He and his wife had found it advisable to pack their bags in late April and join the stream of people heading west. Their wardrobes were still full of clothing and in no time the young soldier was transformed into a civilian. He was extremely appreciative of all the help but after a short stay he said that he would also like to join the exodus to the west since his family lived in Dusseldorf. We never heard from him again.

That day of 2 May was memorable for yet another strange incidence. While my mother was busy transforming the soldier into a civilian, I went outside into the front garden to see if anything else was happening in our road. Suddenly a Jeep drove past on the nearby main road with three soldiers in it who clearly were not Russians. The word spread very quickly that these were actually British soldiers and expectations rose that Rostock would in fact be occupied by British forces and that the Russians would withdraw eastwards again. That was wishful thinking.

As we learnt later, the three British officers had merely driven up to the Town Hall - which by that time was already occupied by the Russian commander - exchanged greetings and drove back westwards again to their own front line.

By the afternoon of the next day Russian soldiers, many of them with Asian or Mongolian features, were swarming all over the town and many of them under the influence of possibly unlimited amounts of alcohol, were forcing their way into houses and apartment in search of valuables - mainly items of gold or watches - and above all in search of female members of the population. Finding truly secure hiding places for mothers and sisters became a major task for most families.

These first few days of May, and the war not having finished officially, were marked by extreme lawlessness and random violence.

It was also during these first few days of May that another tragedy occurred. It happened in the harbour area where Russian solders had accidentally or with intent fired their guns at two stationary railway tank wagons. Apparently the tanks contained fuel for rockets but the Russian soldiers mistook the liquid for something alcoholic and started drinking it as it poured out of the bullet holes in the tanks.

Eye witnesses later reported that within a short time many of the soldiers were writhing in agony and several of them died.

The Russian retribution was swift and brutal. The following day 15 civilian men were randomly apprehended, marched to the main square in front of the town hall and executed by firing squad. War and its brutality was still very much the rule of the day.

Two days after this tragic event and with the country still officially at war, I went down to the harbour, accompanied by two school friends. Rumours were circulating that several naval vessels, among which was also a submarine, were still well-stocked with provisions and other items of interest to young boys. And this turned out to be very true. Apart from a variety of tinned foodstuffs I also found a pair of very impressive naval binoculars in one of the ship's lockers. This was a highly prized find and I only parted with them years later when we made our escape to the West. I really would have loved to take the binoculars with me but they were quite heavy and could also have become an incriminating item in case we were stopped and searched during our escape to Berlin.

This expedition to the harbour also gave me the one and only opportunity to explore the interior of a submarine. I had always had the impression that everything inside these vessels was narrow and cramped and was surprised to find that there was ample space for moving around.

When a few days later - it was in fact the day the war officially came to an end - I returned to the harbour on my own to look for more booty, Russian sentries had now barred access to all the ships.

As the days went by unarmed Russian soldiers began to appear in the streets, many of them laden with booty of various kinds. Wristwatches were particularly prized and I saw one such soldier with possibly eight or ten watches strapped to one arm with the sleeve of his tunic rolled up to give his loot a good public viewing. Their ignorance of values led some enterprising civilians to start bartering with these soldiers and I heard that in some cases solid gold watches were willingly exchanged by the soldiers for cheap but flashier ones. Alarm clocks also became a favoured barter item.

The question most occupying our minds was the whereabouts of our father. He had left in late February for somewhere near Schwerin and we had telephone contact with him right to the end of April, but then the whole telephone service had suddenly become dysfunctional and we had no further communications. It was therefore an enormous relief to all of us when one of my father's colleagues came round to inform us that our father was safe and on his way back to Rostock. And sure enough, a few days later our father arrived with the extra bonus for him that he could now - for the first time - see his recently born son Dietmar, who had arrived just in time to be called a 'war baby'. It was a good feeling to know that we were a reunited family again.

Did your father not express concern that the new occupying powers might wish to question him about his activities under the previous regime?

I am sure he discussed this with my mother, but in our presence no such fears were ever expressed.

The day after his return our father resumed his previously held position at the local administration centre of the Post Office, which happened to be just a short distance away from the Gymnasium at the Rosengarten. Back at work, our father was given the added overall responsibility of restoring at utmost speed the regional telecommunications network, which had also become dysfunctional as a result of bombing raids and deliberate destruction by retreating German forces.

The now-ruling Russian military administration left no-one in doubt that they wanted this service restored without delay.

One day, when my father had joined me on my way to school and we were walking along the Wallgraben, parallel with the old town wall, he pointed at a narrow footpath leading to what looked like a small concrete air-raid shelter.

"This is where I was working," he said, "when I had to leave you all alone at home."

I cannot remember the actual date - it may have been late July or early August because the school holiday had already started - when a colleague of my father came to our home late in the evening. The two of them went into our sitting room and firmly closed the door. After only a few minutes they reappeared again with the colleague bidding his farewell and leaving in great haste. Now my father and my mother locked themselves in the sitting room and as subsequent events showed, it led to a dramatic change in our family's life. My mother reappeared looking rather tearful and when she started packing a suitcase for my father we youngsters realised that something extraordinary must have happened. My father took me briefly aside merely to say that he has been called away again and that he would be in touch with us very shortly. After embraces and an almost sombre goodbye, my father left that very same night and it was only two weeks later that we heard from him again. He had managed to get to Berlin where he had sought shelter with some distant family relatives who lived in a sector of the city occupied by the Western Powers.

Quite dramatic events. No doubt you will enlarge as to why your father had to resort to such a hasty departure.

Indeed I will. It was several years later that I really got to know the full story, because even my mother had not been given the full background prior to my father's hasty departure. I think my father deliberately withheld detailed information from her so that she could genuinely claim not to know anything in case she was subjected to any interrogation.

Early that evening the partially restored central telephone exchange, which was housed in the Post Office Administration centre, had been broken into, severely vandalised and neighbouring rooms set on fire. The restoration work carried out under my father's supervision was more or less wiped out and the whole incident had the hallmark of a deliberate act of sabotage.

The likelihood of my father being held responsible for this act or at least being charged with inadequate security arrangements was very high, particularly as the local Russian army commander had personally demanded that the regional telephone network be restored as quickly as possible. The dispensing of justice would at this stage undoubtedly have been by a Military Tribunal and in these early post-war days, with memories of the only recently concluded hostilities still very much alive, a proper judicial process could not be expected. These must have been the immediate conclusions my father reached after that evening visit by his colleague, which then also led to his decision to leave Rostock in great haste and, if possible, to seek refuge in the West.

After my father's escape we feared that our mother might be summoned to answer questions but fortunately it never happened. The team of repair technicians must have worked feverishly to repair the damage because two weeks later our own telephone line was functioning again and it appears the whole incident was hushed up.

With our father no longer around as the family bread-winner, our financial situation soon became quite precarious. Luckily, just before the war started, one of my father's tasks had been the extension of telephone connections to rural locations in the Rostock surroundings. In the course of his work my father developed friendly relationships with a number of farmers and estate owners. It was always a special treat when my father allowed me to accompany him on his tours of inspection in his little red DKW Post Office car.

These connections now proved to be of immense value. Most of my father's old contacts had to make regular deliveries to the Russian occupying forces and also to some of the emerging civic communist institutions. Dates and meeting places were arranged by telephone and we were truly grateful for the eggs, vegetables and occasional side of meat, which my father's friends managed to 'lose' and which ended up in our larder. The largest single item were potatoes, which in one form or another formed part of our daily meals.

Had civic functions ceased to exist or was there still a basic infrastructure in existence?

Yes, gas and electricity were available, the hospitals did their work as before, trains were still running and even postal services began to function again. A limited number of shops also started to offer a very basic range of foodstuffs again. Overall, however, the return to some form of civic order was slow. The new communist administrators, many of whom were returnees from the Soviet Union after having fled Germany prior to and during the Hitler years, had very little administrative experience. In addition, it seemed they were more occupied with spreading their new dogma rather than dealing with the immediate economic problems of the population.

The new administration, however, lost no time in trying to hunt down members of the previous regime. The fear of the 'knock on the door' was widespread and we felt for some time it could also happen to us in view of our father's departure. Rumours were circulating that victims of these purges were deported east, possibly to Siberia, without being given the opportunity of any judicial processes. An acquaintance of our family, who lived just a few houses away from us, committed suicide by shooting himself when communist officials came to take him away.

Initially, but only for a short period, the new administration allowed the old school curricula to continue. In November, however, several classes including my own were transferred to another school building in the Friedhofs Weg, which happened to be near to the school where I had started my primary education.

Now the new rulers showed their true colours and a new form of mind-manipulation and intimidation began, described as re-education. Firstly we were given several new teachers. The teaching of Latin continued but ancient Greek was discontinued and replaced by Russian. While we had no choice but to attend those classes, most of us old Gymnasiasts expressed our annoyance by continually achieving only minimum passes in our exams and largely ignoring homework. Our old history teacher had to perform a 100% turnaround by explaining to us and praising the achievements of the heroes of Marxism and Communism, such as Engels, Liebknecht, Rosa Luxemburg and others. Lenin featured especially large in all this, but then we had heard of him before in our old history books as the person responsible for bringing about the ending of hostilities in the East, leading to the Peace Treaty of Brest-Litovsk in early 1918 between Russia and Germany.

Until now my class had consisted almost entirely of boys from middle-class families. Suddenly we were infiltrated by numerous boys who came from families with regime-loyal backgrounds. Very quickly the whole atmosphere in the classroom and in fact throughout the school became one of fear and mistrust. The new pupils seemed to be looking constantly for opportunities to report on any remarks by our teachers which could be construed as criticism of our new communist masters or the occupying forces.

In many ways, efforts to achieve the unquestioning submission of the citizen to the dogma of the ruling regime had not changed at all.

I read somewhere that in those early post-war months the Allied Powers and also the Soviet Union made use of all available media channels to remind the population of the atrocities committed under the Hitler regime.

That is correct and is a topic I was about to bring up.

As a result of the bombing raids Rostock had lost most of its cinemas apart from the large cinema in the Breite Strasse. One morning several classes of our school were marched off to this cinema not knowing why and what we were supposed to see.

I have to admit I was genuinely horrified by what we had to watch on the screen. It must have been a documentary film made by the Russians very soon after liberating Auschwitz and Birkenau, to which they had added films captured from the German camp guards. This was then followed by films about the horrendous sufferings of the Russian population during the past four years.

All my fellow pupils were truly filled with shock and horror with what they had just seen and none of us thought that this was just a fabricated piece of communist propaganda, but was a sad and shameful page in our nation's history.

For many of us it was the beginning of accepting our new rulers more sympathetically, particularly as their own atrocities had at this stage not yet become public knowledge.

After seeing these films I remember confronting my mother, asking her to tell me truthfully to what extent she and my father had been aware of these gruesome events prior to and during the war and in particular of the existence of those horrific death camps. She conceded that the public maligning of Jewish citizens had been evident from the early days of the Hitler regime, but when this had culminated in the violent attacks on Jewish shops and the burning of the synagogue in Rostock in November 1938, she and my father were utterly appalled by the brutal treatment unleashed upon our fellow citizens. She said that she was very upset when - shortly after the attacks - she went into town to see numerous shop windows smashed and in particular those of the shoe shop whose owner was a family friend and where my first pair of shoes were bought.

The Kristallnacht, she added, received wide coverage in the national and international press and the atrocious treatment of our Jewish fellow citizens did not remain a secret neither nationally nor internationally. They all had their plush embassies in Berlin and Potsdam and were direct witnesses to the events unfolding in Germany, she said, and they all looked away.

I believed her when she told me that she, my father, and probably millions of ordinary citizens were not aware of the Final Solution, the result of which I had just witnessed in the cinema and I was willing to accept that the rounding-up of Jewish fellow citizens was genuinely, albeit naively, seen by many people as part of a major resettlement scheme in Eastern Europe.

"Do not forget," she said, "that also many non-Jewish citizens suffered under the doctrinaire regime which did not tolerate any form of criticism. We never told you at the time, because you were too young, but your father and I were very upset when Father Leffers, who baptised you in 1934, was arrested the following year and imprisoned for years. Several prominent Rostock citizens and academics had also disappeared during those years of 'nationalistic renewal' and had also become the victims of an all-controlling and invasive regime with its ever-present and relentless propaganda machine."

Presumably at that time you were not aware that the atrocities had occurred on a much larger scale than what you had just witnessed and in many more locations than at Auschwitz.

Yes, it took a few more years before I really got a fuller picture of what had happened. To this very day I ask myself how a supposedly educated population could have closed their eyes to these atrocities, many of them perpetrated in locations close to or surrounded by large conurbations. Could it have been that, as the war intensified and with the civilian population becoming more and more the main victim of this conflict, that their own suffering and endurance had reached a level where their capacity for compassion had been completely numbed and even evil was no longer recognised? To all this I shall most likely never find a satisfactory answer.

After this digression let me return to our life in Rostock.

Unlike the previous regime, the Communists did not make membership of their Youth Organisations (FDJ and Young Pioneers) compulsory, at least not at this early stage, but not joining up voluntarily meant virtual exclusion from recreational activities and it was implied that later accession to universities and jobs in the civil service may not be available. Virtually all my new fellow pupils from regime-loyal families joined the Pioneers: all but one of my longstanding fellow pupils stayed away.

The deserted apartment next door to ours, which had played such an important role in helping a soldier not to end up in Siberia, had remained unoccupied for quite some time. This was surprising, considering the pressure for accommodation from bombed-out families and displaced people from German territories in the East. Then, in early autumn, the apartment must have come to the attention of the local Russian Quartermaster. My mother suspected the informant to be the tenant of another apartment in our house, who as a previous devoted supporter of the Hitler regime now tried to ingratiate himself with the new administration.

Suddenly, one afternoon a lorry turned up outside the house and soldiers started unloading a few boxes and suitcases. They entered the building and demanded the key for the next-door apartment. Soon afterwards a soldier in a rather smart uniform appeared and introduced himself in well-spoken German.

I cannot remember his name but he was a medical doctor from Leningrad, who in the early '30s had been a student at Berlin University. Accompanying him was a rather scruffy soldier with far-eastern features, who turned out to be the doctor's batman. Communications with this individual were confined to sign language and even that led to numerous precarious situations. Thankfully, these could always be sorted out peacefully when the doctor returned from his duty in the evening.

One very precarious situation occurred when the batman returned one afternoon with a dead goat over his shoulder. He must have gutted the animal already at whatever location he got it and rather than have him butcher the rest of the animal upstairs in the apartment, we showed him the large communal wash house on the lower ground floor. Lothar and I stayed with him in the hope of him giving us a pound or two of meat for our family. His butchering was a gruesome spectacle but in the end he managed to get most of it into manageable sizes, all of them looking rather bloody.

Next to the wash house was a small water closet. Not having used it for some time, I pulled the cord just to see if the tank above had filled up with water. It was full but my test had also attracted the attention of the batman.

After disposing of the waste by simply throwing it over the garden fence he returned to the wash house, where he took a piece of blood-stained meat, put it into the bowl of the water closet and having seen me pulling the cord, now did the same. Clearly in his part of the Soviet Union water closets were unheard of.

To this day, I can still see his face, showing firstly bewilderment and then rage. When the flush had settled and he saw the empty bowl he burst into a tirade of what must have been strong Russian swear-words and looking at us he muttered something like "Sabotage Germanski".

It was a day when we really wished for the earliest possible return of the doctor.

Peace was soon restored and the batman looked almost a little apologetic. In the end we received a few pieces of really fresh goat meat safely cleaned up in the apartment's kitchen sink. We had never had goat meat in our family before and I have to admit - in days of little to eat - it tasted particularly good.

The batman, we assumed, had now also learnt not to use the toilet in future for a quick wash.

The doctor stayed in the apartment until early spring the following year. His mere presence in the building had protected us all from troublesome incursions in addition to which we received the occasional small gift of some sugar and flour. His most important contribution, however, was that he helped to correct the deeply engrained perception of the 'Brutal Bolshevic' which the previous regime had so eagerly tried to instil in us.

The new occupants of the apartment were a displaced family of four from West Prussia and - being newcomers to our town - they had to struggle even harder than us to find sustenance above the meagre supplies now beginning to appear in the re-opened shops.

Unfortunately our own source of extra supplies from my father's rural friends had nearly come to an end as the owners of the estates and large farms became victims of the 'Land Reform' and their lands were broken up into Collective Farms. This was supposed to copy the Kolchose type of agriculture as practised in the Soviet Union.

It was many years later that I discovered that my friendly 'Grossbauer' in Broock had also been driven off his farm.

He Who Dares Sometime Wins

※

During all this time, did your father manage to make contact with his family?

Yes, at the end of May we received a very brief note from our father, which strangely enough had been posted in East Berlin, informing us that he had secured safe transport out of Berlin and that the German Post Office had a vacant post for him in the town of Freiburg. We also learnt that my paternal grandparents who had been expelled from their home in Leobschütz in Upper Silesia had survived the harsh conditions of their journey to the West and that they had been resettled in a village called Breitenbach. The fate of our other relations was still unknown.

Since our local newspapers and radio stations concentrated exclusively on promoting our new regime, people had to rely heavily on hearsay and rumours about happenings in the wider world and in particular in the western part of our country. One such rumour was that in the western occupied zones foodstuffs of all kinds were becoming available again.

I knew that very good family friends from Rostock had resettled in Lübeck and then there were also our relations in Hamburg, who we knew had survived the inferno of July 1943.

When the summer holiday came I felt very tempted to venture west to Lübeck, to visit my old friend Christian and above all bring back some food for the family.

It took a considerable time to convince my mother that as a twelve-and-a-half-year-old I would be fit enough and capable of making such a journey west all on my own, particularly as it meant having to cross an increasingly guarded border. Very reluctantly my mother finally agreed after I had explained to her that my experiences as an evacuee boy and my training in the Jungvolk should help me if I encountered difficult situations.

The actual geographical demarcation of that new border was still not very well known but I had heard that an official - albeit heavily guarded - border crossing point existed on the outskirts of Lübeck, near a village called Schlutup. With my mother accompanying me to the station and with only a rucksack as my baggage, we bought a ticket to Wismar. Once in Wismar my plan was to buy a new ticket to Schönberg which would take me close to the border.

It was on this last phase of the train journey that I first noticed the presence of soldiers on the station platforms.

At my end destination I was lucky to find a bus which was heading in the direction of the official border crossing-point but I decided to disembark well before there as I was sure that as a young boy, travelling on his own, I would have aroused the immediate suspicion of any policeman or border guard during an inspection of the travellers on the bus.

Luckily, as I continued west on foot, I met a farmer who kindly gave me a lift on his horse-drawn cart, laden with sheaves of harvested wheat. It very much reminded me of my days back in Broock.

The farmer seemed friendly and I took the risk of confiding in him that I was trying to get over the border to friends in Lübeck, but then to return to my family in Rostock. He took me all the way back to his farm, at which stage I still was not entirely sure whether he was genuinely friendly or whether he would hand me over to the border guards. Thankfully my fears were unjustified.

The farm was indeed very close to the border and with his thorough knowledge of the area the farmer even suggested a route for a night crossing, which he told me was rarely patrolled by the guards. He said that he also had fields on the western side of the border and that he had a special pass to work on those fields. He also mentioned that Russian and East German controls were very severe and any attempt to cross the border in the immediate vicinity of the crossing point was to be avoided. I proved the farmer wrong, but I will come back to that later.

The route recommended by the farmer meant passing

the edge of a lake and an adjoining swamp. He warned me that the footpath, which in part consisted of wooden planks, was very narrow and that I must take extreme care in the dark not to lose my footing. When we stepped outside his house he pointed at two large trees on the western horizon.

"Head for those trees," he said, "and when you get there you will already see the lake. Keep to the right of the lake where you will find the footpath which takes you all the way across the border. The nights are very light now and in any case, you will see the glow in the night sky over Lübeck."

With the onset of dusk I finally set off, full of trepidation and still not absolutely sure if the farmer had not simply set a trap for me. Why was he being so helpful?

I approached the two trees very cautiously, fearing that a border guard might be hiding there but all was quiet and exactly as the farmer had described. The lake appeared right in front of me and its northern shore was only a short distance away. I spotted the footpath immediately. It was easy travelling from here on. I soon reached some houses and public roads on the western side and rested in a bus shelter. When, finally, other people arrived I asked them how to get to the address of my friend and was pleased to hear that they lived not very far away.

I can still remember the astonishment on Christian's mother's face when she opened the door. Christian had been my closest school friend at the Gymnasium in

Rostock and through us, the two families also became good friends. Christian's father, Mr Tischer, had been a lecturer at the Rostock University. In April 1945, however, the family - like so many others - had moved westwards, and fortunately for me they had only moved to close-by Lübeck.

After getting myself cleaned up and eating a wholesome breakfast, I went with Christian for a look round the city, which to my surprise had also suffered a great deal of destruction.

I spent an enjoyable day with the Tischer family and many questions were thrown at me about life in Rostock under the communist regime, how we coped without my father, the whereabouts of friends and acquaintances, what happened to our school and the teachers … just to mention a few.

After dinner Christian's father mentioned that dealers of coins and stamps in Lübeck and possibly also elsewhere in the Western Occupied Zones seemed to be very interested in the new postal stamps issued by the different provinces and even individual towns in the Soviet Occupied Zone. The early issues from Mecklenburg seemed to be of particular interest. I was surprised by this, because in my view they were of extremely poor quality, mainly depicting socialist propaganda such as the agrarian land reform - *Junker Land in Bauern Hand*, (Squires' land in Farmers' hands). Some of the stamps did not even have proper perforations and had to be cut out with scissors.

The following day the Tischers filled my rucksack with a variety of delicious foodstuffs and rather than try another night crossing for my return journey, I headed for the nearby official border crossing point at Schlutup. The warning the farmer had given me about the strict controls at this crossing point must obviously have applied to traffic from East to West. On my arrival there was no hold up at the Western checkpoint and I marched on into what was described as no-man's land. On the eastern end of the road I saw two large trucks and a horse-drawn cart heading east undergoing some form of inspection by two border guards. The guards must have had an animated discussion with one of the truck drivers and nobody noticed a young boy sneaking past on the right hand side of the truck and past the checkpoint building. After a relatively short walk away from the border I saw a bus passing on another road and I knew then that in due course I would get transport back to Schönberg and from there back home to Rostock.

By the time I reached Schönberg I had missed the last train to Wismar but the stationmaster kindly allowed me to spend the night in the station waiting room. The rest of the travel was easy and needless to say my mother was truly relieved to see me back home.

You must have been very pleased with yourself to have coped with such a perilous journey.

Yes, it had made me feel so confident that in the summer of the following year I asked my mother again if I could make another trip to Lübeck. Permission was given, again reluctantly, and at the end of August - counting on my previous experience - I set off westwards again.

Bearing in mind what Mr Tischer had told me about Soviet Zone stamps during my last visit, we bought several sheets of different Mecklenburg stamps, wrapped them up in tinfoil and sealed them up in a cardboard tube.

My train out of Wismar was fairly empty and I shared my compartment with only one other passenger, a woman in her late twenties or early thirties. After what seemed a long silence she asked me I lived in this part of the country and if I was on my way home.

When I told her that I was actually from Rostock and that I was on my way to visit relatives in this area she felt encouraged to tell me more about herself. I had already noticed from her accent that she was not from this part of Germany and as it turned out she was a refugee from East Prussia who in early 1945 had been resettled in Rostock. This broke the ice between us. Very quickly she confided in me that she was trying to get to the West because she had received information that her husband had been taken prisoner by the British and that after his eventual release she would prefer to settle down somewhere in the West.

I now also opened up to her and told her that I was heading west myself, to Lübeck, to obtain provisions and then to return to my family in Rostock. When I asked her to let me see her train ticket I discovered that it had been booked all the way to Schönberg, just like my own.

When I mentioned that I had done a border crossing before, she immediately asked me if she could accompany me. I did not give an immediate answer as all sorts of potential problems went through my mind.

Since it had been my plan to use the farm again as my starting-off point, what would the farmer's reaction be if I turned up with another person - who also carried a sizeable suitcase with her? There were rumours going around that since last year the control of the border had strongly intensified. Even the description 'Iron Curtain' was used. Was the farm now monitored by the border guards?

Maybe the farmer had been expelled from his farm, since it was right in the border zone. Many thoughts like this went through my mind and my initial conclusion was to say no to her request. But as the train approached our final destination my young male self-esteem must have taken over and I agreed to help.

"My name is Ursula," she said.

Fortunately no police patrols had passed through during the whole journey.

The bus service I had used before still existed. I wondered how many of our fellow passengers had the same plan as us. Once off the bus we walked along a country lane in complete silence, Ursula coping remarkably well with her large suitcase. From an elevated point of the lane I saw a building in the distance which looked very much like the farmhouse of the friendly farmer. And so it was. Provided the farmer and his wife were still on the farm I felt quite confident that he would give me a friendly welcome and let me stay in the barn again. But would he extend such hospitality to yet another stranger? After all, if he was found out to be involved in illegal people-trafficking this would have serious consequences for his farm and his family.

With all this on my mind I decided not to let Ursula accompany me right onto the farm. Not far from the building were some shrubs and bushes on the side of the lane.

"Keep yourself hidden here until I come back for you with the onset of darkness," I said.

Not knowing what or whom you would find on the farm, I guess you must have approached it with some fear and trepidation.

That is putting it mildly. It was a hot day anyway but extra sweat was on my forehead.

I heard some noise from the cow shed which sounded like the voice of the farmer. What a relief! He recognised me immediately and expressed his surprise that I once again wanted to use my holiday time to make such challenging journeys. I felt quite proud to be able to tell him that on my return journey last year, and against his advice, I had managed to slip through the Official Border Crossing Point at Schlutup and that I would try that return route also this time.

I did not however mention the young woman I had left near the farm hiding behind some bushes.

After a warm and sunny day, grey clouds appeared late in the afternoon and it began to drizzle. I told the farmer and his wife a little bit more about life in Rostock and my own family and also heard from them about the heavily increased border controls, before I thanked them once again for their help and hospitality.

Dusk set in very rapidly and instead of heading for the two tall trees I did a little detour back to collect Ursula, who looked a little bedraggled but clearly very pleased to see me again. We walked through the wet fields towards the two trees and along the lakeside, reaching the narrow footpath on which I had so easily made my way west the year before.

As we started out on this narrow path I noticed already that with the rain the latticed stretches had become quite slippery and our progress was slow as Ursula also had to carry her suitcase. Then, three-quarters of the way across and possibly already in West Germany or at least in no-man's land, I lost my footing and fell into the swamp to the right of the path. Ursula, who was right behind me, immediately threw herself flat onto the path and reached out for my hand to stop me from sinking further into the swamp. She proved to be a strong woman and quickly managed to pull me back onto the path. With all the mud on us we both must have been a sight to behold. One niggling question to which I had no instant answer was: had the wrapped-up stamps in my rucksack survived this watery accident?

Not long after this, we saw lights from nearby houses and I knew that we had reached the outskirts of Lübeck again. With the drizzle having turned into a heavy rain, some of the mud was washed off us but when we came across a large puddle by a roadside we both tried to give ourselves a clean-up. It was at this point that Ursula took an envelope out of her suitcase and extracted a bundle of banknotes.

"You have earned them," she said.

As it turned out I was really in her debt for having pulled me out of the swamp.

On our way to a bus shelter Ursula told me that she would be heading for Kiel where she knew some of her relatives had settled after their expulsion from East Prussia. I waited until a bus arrived to take her to the centre of Lübeck and after waving her goodbye I made my way to the Tischers' home. The surprise of seeing me again was written all over their faces, accentuated possibly by seeing me in such a muddy condition. Before I even had a proper clean-up, I was anxious to unwrap the sealed cardboard cartridge. It was a great relief to find that the stamps had safely survived my earlier accident and were completely dry and thus saleable. Christian's father was very impressed that I had followed his advice on my previous visit and he promised to take me to a stamp and coin dealer whom he knew personally. This we did the following morning.

All I knew is what I had paid for the stamps in Rostock but I had no idea what additional collector's value to add to my asking price. After some supportive intervention by Christian's father the dealer gave me two-and-a half-times the face value, which I found to be very satisfactory. He also gave me a note naming a variety of stamps issued by other provinces and towns in eastern Germany, that he said were very popular with collectors in the West.

After another enjoyable day with the Tischer family and Christian telling me all about his new school in Lübeck it was time for me to plan my return journey. Thinking of my easy crossing last year at the official border station I decided to try the same again. Before setting off the next morning I wrote a postcard to my father and not knowing his private address I sent it to the 'Hauptpostamt' – the main post office - in Freiburg. I learnt later that the card actually reached him.

My rucksack was once again full with a variety of delicious provisions and having sold the stamps profitably plus the generous donation from Ursula I had quite a small fortune to take back home. If caught during the border crossing I knew I would lose everything.

This time the checkpoint on the eastern side seemed to be much busier than on my previous crossing. Several large trucks were going from east to west and a long row of agricultural vehicles were going from west to east. There were quite a number of border guards around but they all appeared very busy with climbing in and out of the trucks, examining documents and large sheets of paper, and some of them deeply involved in conversations with the people travelling from west to east. All in all, ideal condition for a young boy just to walk along without being paid any attention. I could hardly believe my luck when I finally slipped through under the barrier and I was back in East Germany.

Luck indeed. It would have needed only one guard to be curious about you and you would have been in serious trouble, particularly with carrying so much money on you.

Yes, you are right. Good fortune was with me once again but then, that is what you need for crossing borders illegally.

After two surprisingly easy crossings at Schlutup I began to think that I might even try to cross westwards at this official border post, should my mother give me permission to make yet another trip west during next year's summer school holidays.

Back in Rostock my mother was again greatly relieved to see me back unharmed and we all enjoyed the things I had purchased in Lübeck including some special tinned baby foods for my youngest brother, Dietmar. My mother was very impressed that I had managed to sell the stamps at such a large profit but I told her that a large part of the money I had brought back was a donation from a person I had helped to cross into West Germany. I did not mention my accident on that slippery footpath, in case it would diminish my chances of her approval for any future journeys to the West.

In 1948 life seemed to return to a more structured pattern, although it became increasingly clear - even to us teenagers - that the growing ideological gap between the East and the West could easily lead to a more permanent division of our country. Snippets of information leaked from the historic conference in Potsdam in 1945 had already revealed that the former enemy nations had very different views about a post-war Germany and with Communism now imposing its ideology over large swathes of eastern and central Europe, Germany was now 'the pig in the middle'.

As you may yourself remember, in June the Soviet Union imposed a complete blockade of Berlin, demonstrating the tensions that now existed between former allies. The border stretching from Czechoslovakia to the Baltic Sea now seemed to become a real 'Iron Curtain'.

With our family being separated and without a breadwinner, my mother had to dig into family savings and sadly also dispose discreetly of several family valuables. This included our piano. Although I had been given my first name after that famous Austrian composer and piano virtuoso, my own mastery of the instrument had remained rather modest, since after my father's departure I had to rely entirely on self-tuition, which became very random and poorly structured. In any case with so many other pressing demands upon us, the piano had not received much attention lately and its departure was readily accepted by all.

One of my father's old farmer friends who had escaped expulsion from his farm paid us an unexpected visit one day with a box full of cabbages and potatoes plus a few eggs. As he was about to leave he suggested to my mother that we should keep a few hens in our own back garden. He could give us two or three hens and a few young chickens. When I heard this, it immediately brought back memories of my happy days on the farm in Broock and I urged my mother to accept the visitor's kind offer.

When I hastily assured my mother that I could find the necessary timber for a hen-house and mesh wire for an enclosure, she rather reluctantly agreed to this new venture.

The procurement of the timber and the roofing felt and above all of the considerable length of mesh-wire fencing became more challenging than I had anticipated and I have to admit that the method of obtaining all the materials was a little questionable.

Within a week and with the help of a family friend, the hen-house was completed and became the proud centrepiece in the hen enclosure.

True to his word the farmer delivered three hens - two white ones and a black one - and five chickens.

My procurement of wooden planks and timber had been so successful that after the completion of the hen-house, I still had quite a lot of material left over. Rather than cutting it up into firewood, as my mother suggested, it occurred to me that it could be turned into a rabbit hutch, thus adding another new dimension to my emerging 'mini farmyard'. I happened to know a family in our road who kept a variety of rabbit breeds. In exchange for a few items from our larder we were promised three young ones from a recent litter and after reassuring our mother that the main purpose was to keep the rabbits as pets and not as a potential supplement to our dinner table, she agreed to this project.

The building of the rabbit hutch turned out to be more difficult than I had foreseen with individual meshed doors for each hutch.

Three young rabbits duly arrived together with a sack full of straw and our days of animal husbandry had begun.

The mini farmyard, as you call it, must have prevented you from partaking in many of the usual hobbies and activities which young boys of your age enjoy.

I didn't really miss not playing football or handball or other field sports or swimming. Looking after the animals provided much pleasure to all of us. Furthermore we also had a small allotment in Reutershagen which required attention by all available hands. The procurement of healthy foodstuffs of any kind remained the 'leitmotif' of our daily life.

It must have been around this time that my attention was drawn to yet another potential source of food for the family table. I remembered that my father had kept a fishing rod together with a box of hooks, swivels and reel of fishing lines in the attic of the house. Next to the fishing rod I also found a tall leather bag containing six thin aluminium tubes which could be joined together to make a very long thin lightweight rod. My mother told me that our father had used these tubes as a test antenna when he worked for the Post Office. The actual fishing rod was clearly only a casting rod but my father's test antenna would make a good long rod for mackerel fishing off the pier at Warnemünde. I had seen other anglers there before and had noticed their very long fishing rods.

To give my test antenna the appearance of a fishing rod I added a length of cane to the top end. Having seen that the anglers used hooks dressed merely with white feathers I prepared a number of hooks myself, having ample supply of white feathers from our two white hens.

When I unpacked my aluminium tubes on the pier I got strange looks from the other anglers, who all seemed to have beautiful long cane rods.

I only caught three mackerel that day but they were a tasty and nutritious addition to the family dinner table.

When I mentioned my fishing experience to a school friend, he asked me to accompany him one day for eel fishing in the river Warnow. He told me to come just by myself - with no fishing rod, lines or hooks - but to tell my mother that I would most likely be very late coming home, because the best time for catching them was often only after sun set.

The day we met up my friend also had no fishing rod but merely an old cigar box in which he had several length of fishing line with many hooks attached to them.

On the way down to the river's edge, he cut a few sticks from hazelnut bushes and I was beginning to wonder how all this would end. Down at the water's edge he produced a tin from his pocket: the tin was filled with small pieces of smelly meat that he then used for baiting the hooks. He then tied the baited line to the bottom end of two hazelnut sticks, which he then - a few metres apart - pushed into the soft bottom of the riverbed.

"That is it," he said. "Now we wait."

I have to admit that mackerel fishing was definitely more exciting than sitting here among the reed grasses waiting for something to happen down below in the slightly murky waters of the river. Soon after sunset my friend decided to pull up the hazelnut sticks and to my amazement two eels had indeed taken the bait and were now writhing around the lines and hooks. My friend was certainly well prepared for this catch as he quickly pulled a small cotton bag from his trouser pocket to give him a firm grip on these slimy creatures and to bag them for our return home. He regarded it as a good outing and we shared the catch between us. My mother looked upon it as a rare delicacy and never mentioned my very late homecoming.

I have to admit that I did not go eel fishing again until many years later.

With two more weeks still available until the end of the summer break, I suggested to my mother that I could make another trip west and visit my mother's cousin and her husband in Hamburg. She was very hesitant.

Did I realise, she said, that there was now a different currency in the West? That the political tension was growing day by day and border controls probably stricter than ever?

"In addition you will miss your cousin Edeltraud who is coming from Zwickau to spend a brief holiday with us," she added.

"As you know from the previous trips," I responded, "they only last two to three days and I am sure, that the crossing I have used twice now, is still safe."

It was quite a struggle to get my mother's approval.

Following the earlier success with the sale of Mecklenburg postal stamps in Lübeck, I decided to try the same again for my trip to Hamburg. I had kept the note from the Lübeck stamp dealer that mentioned the issues of particular interest to West German private collectors. To obtain these issues from Sachsen, Thueringen, the Leipzig Fair and also Berlin I went to see a stamp and coin dealer by the name of Mantow in the Blut Strasse in Rostock who luckily had a number of these stamps readily available. Together with several sheets of Mecklenburg stamps I once again filled up a cardboard cartridge and sealed it securely.

My mother also gave me a piece of jewellery for her cousin in Hamburg and a letter to my father which I said I would post to the Hauptpostamt in Freiburg as I had done with previous mail to him.

Having by now become quite familiar with travelling towards the border area, I once again set off for Wismar and then on to Schönberg. The whole journey was quite uneventful. I was very pleased to see that the old bus route to the official border checkpoint was still functioning and I think even the driver was still the same man as on my last trip. Soon after leaving Schönberg, however, I noticed the presence of uniformed border guards at some of the bus stops and also several vehicles passing our bus with uniformed personnel in them. It did not require much guessing that security measures in the border zone had strongly increased, something my mother had already alluded to prior to my departure.

After leaving the bus a little earlier than I had done the year before, I started walking in what I hoped to be the right direction for the farmhouse.

I had walked for about half an hour, with many doubts going through my mind, when I saw a horse-drawn cart coming down a lane, stacked high with sheaves of dry wheat or barley. I could hardly believe it when the man sitting on the top of his load turned out to be my friendly farmer. He was truly surprised to see me again. He climbed down from the top of his cart and looked up and down the lane as if in fear of something. He told me that security throughout the region had been stepped up and that for two days every week a border guard was now stationed on his farm. He thought that the footpath along the lakeside and the swamp still provided a safe crossing.

"I do not expect the border guard to be on my farm today," he said, "but recently, guards have been patrolling lanes and fields along the border."

He feared that I might not be able to accompany him unnoticed back to the farm. I told him then that I had not intended to go back to Lübeck but to visit relatives in Hamburg.

When he heard this I remember him saying: "Well, young man, you have covered nearly half the distance - you might as well finish the job."

With that he climbed back onto his cart, pulled out a few sheaves from his neatly stacked load and then beckoned me to join him up there. He told me to crouch into the space where he had just removed the sheaves and having done so he placed the sheaves loosely over me. The farmer seated himself just in front of my hiding place and we proceeded towards the farm building. The need for this extra security quickly became apparent.

Shortly before reaching the farm I heard a voice ordering the farmer to stop and to come down from his cart. From then on I could only hear muffled voices followed by a longish silence while we remained stationary. Finally I heard the farmer climbing up again to the top of his load and he almost placed himself on top of me.

It was about an hour later, on the farm, that I was given the full story of that encounter on the lane.

A border guard had suddenly appeared out of nowhere and had told the farmer to stop his cart. After having asked the farmer for his personal identification, the guard then apparently produced a long telescopic steel rod and walked round the cart, pushing the rod randomly into the stacked sheaves of wheat. It was only after this procedure that the farmer was allowed to continue on his drive back to the farm.

It occurred to me that the farmer must have gone through a similar form of control before, which explained why he had created the hiding place for me at the top of his load. I expressed my sincere thanks to him for having had such a foresight.

"Had you been found," he said, "it would have had nasty consequences for me too."

Although I felt a great temptation to do so, I never told the farmer that on my previous trip I had actually helped a young woman across the border and that I lost my footing on that footpath.

With the first sign of dusk I bade my farewell, not realising at that moment that this was to be my last encounter with this friendly and helpful farmer and his wife.

As in the past I headed for my landmark, the two tall trees, but as I approached them I passed what looked like a freshly dug hole in the ground. I looked into this hole and to my horror I noticed a small yellow glimmer at the bottom of it.

I crouched down to take closer look and suddenly got a faint whiff of tobacco smoke. It was a cigarette-end, still burning. I stood up again seriously expecting a border guard to be standing right behind me, but I was still all on my own. Surely the person who must have dropped that still burning cigarette could not be far away? I stood still, listening for any movement around me, but all was still. Was the guard now hiding behind those two trees? I still do not know to this day what drove me forward to continue with my journey. I soon reached the familiar footpath and after a trouble-free walk and the glow of the Lübeck lights ahead of me, I reached West German soil again.

I arrived at the Lübeck Central Station early in the morning looking for a train to Hamburg. Since my last journey west, however, a significant change had taken place: the introduction of the West Mark. The conductor on the bus to the station kindly let me have a free ride but at the railway station the clerk at the counter insisted that he could only accept West Marks for my ticket to Hamburg.

He pointed me in the direction of a money-changing office in the station where, to my surprise, I found myself joining two other travellers who found themselves in the same predicament.

With my crisp new West Marks I bought my first railway ticket in West Germany.

I was no newcomer to seeing the destruction from wartime air-raids but what I saw now in Hamburg exceeded all my previous experiences. I remembered our overnight stop in Hamburg in July 1943 and the devastation around the Central Station but I had no idea that further raids that same week had caused destruction of an unimaginable scale. My relatives lived in Hamburg Altona and to my horror large parts of this district were still just a heap of rubble interspersed with many ghostly shells of burnt-out houses. Large diggers and earth-moving machinery were busy working on numerous sites. The roads appeared to be clear, with public and private transport flowing freely; pedestrians moved around sometimes disappearing into houses that looked far too damaged to be inhabitable. I wondered what the home of my relatives would be like.

When I finally got to their address, thanks to the help of passing pedestrians, I found a narrow footpath leading up to what appeared to be the skeleton of a burnt-out house. The ground floor, however, had an attractive wooden door and a curtained window next to it.

I received a wonderful welcome from my aunt Lotte and her husband Peter and was amazed to see how they had turned the ground floor of this severely damaged house into quite comfortable living quarters with access to both electricity and water and even a telephone line. We talked way into the night, bringing our family histories up to date in the course of which we also had to accept that in numerous cases, particularly on my paternal side, the whereabouts and fate of several relatives were still unknown.

My mother's gift was gratefully received and when I told them that I had a cartridge full of East German stamps, hoping to find an interested dealer here in Hamburg, Uncle Peter told me that one of his work colleagues was a fanatical stamp collector who no doubt could recommend such a dealer to us. We received a recommendation the following day. Uncle Peter was a train driver with the Reichsbahn, the German State Railway Company where drivers worked on a roster programme. Fortunately my visit had just coincided with his days off from work and he accompanied me on my visit to the dealer.

As it turned out, the dealer was very enthusiastic about the selection of stamps I had brought and offered me straight away four times the face value in new West Marks. I accepted and began to think that trading in stamps could become quite an enjoyable and profitable hobby.

I posted my mother's letter to our father in Freiburg together with a brief note of my own explaining my presence in Hamburg and informing him that our relatives, although bombed-out, were alive and well.

I spent three wonderful days with my aunt and uncle who went out of their way to show me around this huge city. In spite of the horrendous destruction suffered only a few years earlier, there was a feeling of vibrancy and activity wherever we went, very different from the atmosphere back home in Rostock.

With my rucksack again filled with provisions and quite a few West Marks in my pocket, I was taken by Uncle Peter to the Central Station. Being an employee of the Reichsbahn he was entitled to free travel tickets and he gave me his ticket to Lübeck. I felt quite emotional as I waved him goodbye with the train slowly leaving the station that I will probably always associate with the horrific events in 1943.

On arrival in Lübeck I headed again for the Money Exchange Office and was very pleased to receive almost three times the value of my West Marks.

I presume that at this stage you had already made up your mind on where to cross back into East Germany.

I gave it a lot of thought on my train journey back from Hamburg. Having had two successful crossings at the Schlutup checkpoint in the past, I began to convince myself that I could have another lucky sneak-through.

The bus took me right to the western side of the border crossing where I noticed a much larger presence of uniformed personnel both on the western side and also beyond the no-man's zone on the eastern side. The barriers were down and there was no traffic of any kind.

As I stood there, beginning to think that I should abandon a crossing here and try a return crossing via the footpath along the swamp back to the friendly farmer, an officer came along and asked me why I was standing there all by my own.

I explained to him that my home town was Rostock and

that I would like to get home again but that I had no official papers for a border crossing.

He was a man with a very kindly face and he asked me to follow him to his office. He explained to me that he himself had been a refugee from Silesia and that his own family had been scattered over different parts of Germany after the expulsion from his home region.

"I have been informed, however," he said, "that the authorities on the other side are supportive of the Family Reunification Programme."

He proceeded to fill in a form with my personal details to which he must have added something about me having been separated from my family and wishing to rejoin them. He put it all into an envelope and told me to hand it to the senior officer on the other side of the border.

The relatively short stretch of no-man's land seemed endless. Would it all work?

Would they ask me all sorts of extra questions about the alleged separation from my family? Would they let me keep the contents of my rucksack? Would they ask how and where I had obtained all those Ost Marks? To put it mildly, I was really scared. There was no way back now.

As I approached the eastern barrier one of the border guards told me to walk round the barrier and to follow him. I told him that I had an official letter that I need to hand over personally to the senior officer of the checkpoint. He immediately changed his direction and led me into the administration block where I was presented to a very smartly dressed young officer. After casting his eye over me he opened the letter and after what seemed to be an approving nod he asked the guard to take me to another room. I feared for the worst but after about half an hour of being alone in the room and no one interested in the contents of my rucksack or in doing a body search which would have revealed my substantial sum of money, another guard arrived, took me outside and pointed out where the official bus stop was. I could hardly believe my good fortune.

I came to the conclusion that going from west to east was decidedly easier than east to west.

The rest of the journey back to Rostock was uneventful with no controls going through trains travelling eastwards.

My arrival back home was a cause for celebration by us all and above all a great relief to my mother. My cousin Edeltraud was still with us and took a great interest in hearing about life on the other side of the border. A few days later she travelled back to Zwickau and it was only many years later that I met up with her again in England.

After reflecting upon the latest easy passage through the East German border checkpoint, it occurred to me that my short detention in that room at the border station was probably used by guards to make a telephone call to the Civic Offices in Rostock to establish that a family with my name actually existed and that a positive response had led to my quick and trouble-free release.

During my absence our livestock had been well looked after by my two younger brothers and judging by the number of eggs in the larder, our hens were also performing well.

At school and in the course of our daily lives, we became increasingly aware of the growing hostility to all things western. Newspapers and the radio revelled in decrying western capitalism and highlighting the moral and economic benefits of the new socialist regime. In many of the more densely populated housing areas political cadres were formed whose task it was to educate the mainly adult population about the virtues of a socialist society.

We as youngsters were subjected to this endless indoctrination at school. It was only a few months earlier, you may recall, that this clash of ideologies nearly led to a fresh military conflict when the Russians blockaded Berlin.

Did you get the impression that the population as a whole and the younger generation in particular responded positively to this indoctrination?

I did not know how most of the population reacted to this constant indoctrination but I was able to make some interesting observations among friends, neighbours and my fellow pupils. Friends of our family were, by and large, of a mature age with a few of them having been party members of the previous regime. Many of them were still mourning the loss of sons, brothers and fathers - still reported missing, killed or in Russian camps. On the whole these friends of ours showed a complete indifference to the never-ceasing propaganda. Some people, like one of our neighbours who had also been a NSDAP member, now tried to ingratiate themselves with the new regime by becoming cheer-leaders for our new socialist society. Then of course there were many people who simply followed the new dictat in order to keep their jobs and the ability to carry out their professions. And do remember that many of the hard-line opponents to Russian-style socialism had already fled to the West anyway.

My school provided me with the best insight into attitudes towards our new masters. My own class was rather divided due to the post-1945 infiltration by boys from regime-friendly families, who kept referring to us former Gymnasiasts as outsiders. And so we probably were. Like myself, several of my fellow pupils had not forgotten the horrific films we had to watch in 1945, which had left us all with a lasting feeling of shame and betrayal. Now we saw a new administration using almost identical methods of mind manipulation. We had become 'disbelievers', disillusioned with any form of autocratic government. In the classes below us, I was told, the indoctrination had a much higher success rate.

Being a family without a regular income, my mother became increasingly concerned about our financial situation. Help from my father's old farmer friends had virtually ceased with their estates having been turned into Collective Farms. The sale of some of my mother's jewellery and pieces of family china provided some relief, but we all knew it could not go on for ever. However in this hour of need a letter arrived from our father via our relatives in Berlin informing us about his own situation in Freiburg, his new position with the German Post Office and also a brief confirmation that he had received the mail I had sent from Lübeck and Hamburg. Finally he mentioned that in our cellar we would find two boxes filled with several dozen radio valves. In those days such valves were still a vital part of all radio sets and replacements were most difficult to obtain.

The two boxes were duly located and all valves were still properly boxed and seemed to be in perfect condition. A number of trusted friends and acquaintances were only too willing to pay us handsomely for these valves. For the time being, our finances were once again in a relatively stable condition.

Did your father's letter make any suggestions about a possible reunification of the family?

No, strangely enough, he made no reference to that, presumably for fear of his letter being intercepted and thus exposing us to controls by political cadres or even the police. As I found out much later, my presumption was correct.

Due to our improved finances, Christmas 1948 could be celebrated in a more traditional fashion. A family friend, who we suspected had helped himself to a few trees in the nearby forest, kindly gave us one; my mother brought out her boxes of lametta and my brother Lothar and I used our limited technical skills to set up the model railway system in our sitting room. To top it all, my mother even succeeded in procuring a small carp for our traditional Christmas Eve fish soup. It was a Christmas almost like in olden days, except that we were a divided family.

In his Christmas sermon in the Johannis Church, Pastor Gallay made numerous references to families torn apart in a divided country and it must have given some comfort to my mother to know that we were not alone in this predicament.

In Rostock, civic life seemed to return to some form of normality. Local transport services were beginning to be reliable again, the availability of all sorts of foodstuffs improved significantly and the rebuilding of destroyed buildings had begun with remarkable determination.

Politically, however, the growing tension between East and West - accentuated by the creation of two different currencies - made the fervently desired reunification of our country look more unlikely every day. Rumours circulated that the controls along what was now widely referred to as the Iron Curtain had increased significantly with fencing and even watchtowers and that border crossings had become a very hazardous venture.

Since my mother originated from Zwickau in Saxony, most of my maternal relatives lived in and around that city. Postal services again functioned very well and my aunt Trudel kept us well up-to-date on how they were all coping.

Sadly this included also a message that our grandmother had died. Our mother was deeply shaken by these news as it had been several years since she last saw her mother and the existing circumstances now did not even allow her to attend her funeral in Zwickau.

Contacts with our paternal relations had broken down completely except for a postcard from my grandparents, which contained only the brief information that they had been resettled in a place called Breitenbach in Hessia. Knowing their new location had quite a bearing on a future event that nearly had very dire consequences for me. I shall come back to that later.

It was several months later that I learnt about the sufferings and hardship my grandparents and other close relatives had to endure during their expulsion from their homes in Silesia.

Did they all succeed in getting to West Germany?

Well, in these early post-war years it was still very difficult to obtain a clear picture of what had happened to the individual members of my wider family.

My father's youngest brother Hans, who before the war had been a dentist in Breslau, had been reported missing on the eastern front during the final stages of the war. Was he a prisoner? Was he killed?

His wife and young daughter had joined that horrific

march to the West and finally ended up in that well-known town of Hameln. It was years later that our uncle Hans was finally declared as 'killed'.

Then there was our Uncle Walter who also had the misfortune of being assigned to the eastern front, ending up as a prisoner of war. Thankfully his imprisonment lasted only until 1948 and after his release he traced his wife and daughter to a place in Westphalia where the family was finally reunited. Uncle Walter, who in March 1934 also became my Godfather, was a chartered land surveyor.

After the occupation of northern France in 1940 he was commissioned by the German War Ministry to survey the French coastline for the construction of those massive bunkers and defence installations that later became known as the West Wall. This, however, did not save him from being called up for army service at the end of his work in France. He was also sent to the eastern front where he was taken prisoner in 1944. Thankfully he only had to suffer the Russian camps for four years.

Finally there was our Uncle Erhardt. In his civilian days he had been a bank manager in a small town called Rybnick in Upper Silesia. He had been called up from the very beginning of the war and like his two brothers had the misfortune of being posted to the eastern front where finally he also ended up in captivity.

He only returned from Russia in 1954, a mentally and physically broken man.

He never spoke much about his time in captivity but from the odd comments he made we gathered that conditions in the camp had been so gruesome that inmates even resorted to cannibalism for their survival. After he had rejoined his family and had resettled in Freiburg, he started work again with a local savings bank – however, his already weak health deteriorated further and he passed away four years later. In 1945 his family, our Aunt Herta and his two daughters Ingrid and Christel also had to join what became the largest mass expulsion in modern history, involving - so I was told - nearly 12 million people.

It was only a number of years later that I gathered this information about my paternal relatives, but I thought I would mention it at this stage to let you appreciate the post-war turmoil and traumas affecting our extended family but shared with a vast number of other families.

I have purposely avoided mentioning some of the horrific experiences my relatives suffered on their march west, which I know they tried very hard to erase from their memories.

Thank you very much for this kaleidoscopic summary of your extended family, which provides a general insight into the aftermath of this fateful and devastating conflict.

Now let me get back to our own home in Rostock.

The beginning of 1949 remained rather uneventful.

I had not yet been confirmed into the Lutheran Church and Pastor Gallay suggested one Sunday that I should attend his weekly Bible classes in preparation. My mother supported this suggestion strongly, although she admitted to me that this would no doubt cause some eyebrow-raising by the paternal side of the family, who for many generations had been devoted followers of the Catholic faith.

So, once a week after school I attended these classes together with a small group of other teenagers but also several adults. It was nearly a year later, 2 April 1950 to be precise, that I was confirmed into the Lutheran Church in the presence of my very pleased mother and my brothers Lothar and Dietmar.

Pastor Gallay welcomed me into the Christian community by choosing the words of St John Chapter 15 Verse 16.

Meanwhile the political tension between East and West was reaching a new climax with the official creation of two separate German States. The rhetoric got more hostile day by day and even ardent optimists were beginning to accept that we were to remain a divided nation. With all these events swirling around us, what was the future for our family? Would our father take the risk of returning to Rostock? How much longer could we survive without a proper breadwinner?

In the letter previously mentioned, our father had alluded to some papers and drawings kept in the sideboard in our sitting-room. The mere mention of these papers indicated to us that our father was interested in obtaining them. The papers and drawings were duly found. Being curious by nature I had a look at these drawings but could not make much sense of them except that it had something to do with the manoeuvrability of heavy road vehicles. It crossed my mind at the time that this may have been work related to his short stay at Penemünde and that these drawings may have had something to do with the movement of those heavy V2 rockets that had come into action at the latter stages of the war.

The finding of these papers and drawing led to a very long discussion with my mother. Should we simply ignore this implied request? Should I try to get to Lübeck again and post the papers from there? Should I make the long trek of nearly 1,000 kilometres from Rostock to Freiburg? If so, should I try to get to Lübeck again and then travel from there to Freiburg? Or should I try to travel in East Germany - the German Democratic Republic as it was now called - as far south as possible, paying with East Marks, which would be less expensive?

The outcome of all this was that we decided I should make the long journey to Freiburg by using East German trains right down to the border with Hessia, in the hope of also re-establishing contact with our paternal grandparents in Breitenbach.

We all felt that after such a long separation, it was important that some direct contact with our father should be made and to hear from him personally what his own plans were to get the family reunited.

It took my mother two days to agonise over whether to give her consent to such a hazardous venture and in the end she was probably influenced by the fact that I already had three successful border crossings to my credit.

I spent several days studying maps at home and in the public library. Our own atlas and maps of Germany, whilst good at showing the railway network, did not tell me the exact marking of the East-West border. The new maps in the Public Library, on the other hand, were fully up to date.

It soon became clear that I should head for a town called Eisenach, which was virtually on the border with West Germany and also close to my first target destination of Breitenbach where my paternal grandparents now lived. The map seemed to indicate that at that location the river Werra formed the border between East and West.

Soon after the school summer break had started, I set off on my long journey south, full of doubts as to whether we had made the right decision. Would it not have been much easier to try the familiar crossing to Lübeck again and then make the short journey to Hamburg where my Uncle Peter could probably have obtained a free rail ticket for me to Freiburg? I did not mention any of this to my mother as we drove by tram car to the Rostock railway station. At the station she bought my ticket to Magdeburg. Thereafter I was going to purchase the tickets myself depending on suitable onward connections.

It was another emotional farewell. My mother had raided our larder to fill my rucksack with a variety of delicacies and also a home-baked cake. In anticipation of a river crossing my father's papers were securely protected in a sealed cartridge. It was agreed that I would not carry any letters on me for my father or my grandparents.

The train journey was comfortable, albeit much longer than I had anticipated.

After passing through Schwerin I was still plagued by doubts as to whether I should continue, but at the same time I could not sum up enough courage to get off at the next stop and buy myself a return ticket to Rostock.

After stops at Wittenberge and Stendal the train finally got to Magdeburg. This was my second visit, as some years back in 1943 I had passed through here on my way back from the holiday camp in the Harz Mountains. The arrival in Magdeburg was very late and outward traffic had come to a halt. I decided therefore to spend the night in the station waiting-room where several other adult travellers had settled down for the night. I had just about found a length of bench on which to stretch out when there was the sound of loud footsteps on the outside station platform. "Here come the police again," murmured one of the travellers. My instant reaction was to grab my rucksack and to exit through a back door. As a lone teenager without any identity papers I felt sure I would be a prime target for any policeman.

As I found out later, two policemen came into the waiting

room to check the identity papers of all those present.

That was a lucky escape and at this stage you had only covered a small part of your journey.

Yes, that was indeed a narrow escape and with more than 200 kilometres still ahead of me to my planned border crossing point, I had to be prepared for increased controls and security checks the nearer I got into the border zone.

The following morning I studied my map again to see if the use of secondary railway lines would take me further south, but the search for smaller country towns with railway connections to them and onward travel facilities became so complicated that I finally decided to take the risk of going on a main line all the way to Erfurt.

By now the station waiting room began to fill up with other travellers and I left to study the departure board for trains to Erfurt. The station hall was full of people, among them several in Volkspolizei uniform and also some Russian soldiers.

The departure board showed three separate trains for Erfurt and judging by the number of stops shown, two of these trains were bound to be very slow. Were they the ones less likely to be patrolled by the police? Or was the early fast train to Erfurt a safer bet?

I had a look at the fast train standing already on the platform and saw people boarding the coaches. They all looked like well-dressed civilians. No police in sight. I quickly rushed back to the ticket office and bought my ticket for Erfurt.

The compartment was already occupied by a man and a woman, who had taken up the window seats. They both looked curiously at my rucksack but also gave me a reassuring smile. After an hour or so the man asked me if I was going home or visiting friends in Erfurt.

"Yes, I am spending some of my school break with relatives," I replied.

Having heard me speak he knew that I was not from these parts of Germany and I added that I had come all the way from Mecklenburg.

He then told me that he himself was from Halle in Saxony and that he was an accountant on an inspection tour of HO shops, the government-owned chain of retail outlets for a wide range of consumer goods.

He soon occupied himself again with looking at sheets of paper and I retreated into my comfortable corner to catch up with some extra sleep. I only awoke when the door was flung open and a friendly train conductor asked to see our tickets. The woman in the compartment never spoke and spent all the time busily knitting a scarf or some form of longish garment.

The train finally pulled into Erfurt Station by the middle of the afternoon and I had survived the whole comfortable journey without a single control by police or border guards. My fellow traveller, the accountant, wished me a happy holiday and as I said that my relatives lived a distance outside Erfurt he kindly gave me the directions to the central bus station.

I was beginning to feel much more at ease with this whole venture.

At the bus station I saw a coach marked for Gotha, which I knew would take me even more westwards towards the border and with early evening approaching and this being the last coach for the day I quickly decided to board.

Gotha turned out to be a very elegant town with no evidence of having suffered any damage during the war. With dusk setting in, where could I spend the night? The nearby railway station might once again provide shelter in the waiting room, but when I finally got there the doors were firmly locked. I noticed, however, that outside the station - just a short distance away - were two coaches on what looked to be an obsolete track. With no railway staff in sight I made my way to these two coaches and on entering one of them it became clear that they were in need of a complete overhaul. Some of the windows were broken, seats were missing, shards of glass were lying about and there was a general presence of debris of various kinds. One thing was for sure: no locomotive would come during the night and pull these two coaches away.

Fortunately I found a length of seating long enough to stretch out on and I had a shelter for yet another night.

Early the next morning I sneaked back into the station, firstly for a personal clean-up but also to check how best to proceed towards the border. Eisenach was now only a short distance away, but as it was a significant town on the border I began to fear that even entering this town would be hazardous due to extra-stringent controls.

I had another thorough look at my map and noticed a small village called Creuzburg just a few kilometres north of Eisenach and right on the border with the river Werra, being the actual East-West divide. Creuzburg, however, had no railway connection, which made the decision for me. I had to continue by local bus services. At the bus station I studied the various routes available and found to my surprise that with one bus change at another village I could actually get to Creuzburg within two or three hours. I departed on the first available bus and to my relief there were no uniformed persons amongst my fellow travelers. I had a comfortable seat at the back of the bus and found myself marveling at the hilly and wooded countryside through which we passed.

Creuzburg turned out to be a much smaller village than I had expected, but on arrival I immediately noticed several uniformed border guards sharing a table outside a shop, clearly enjoying a drink. Nobody paid any attention to me as I passed them. A few minute later I saw someone who looked like a local person and I asked in which direction the river was.

Being now in completely unfamiliar territory I decided to hide my rucksack in some dense shrubs and to explore the access route to the river for a possible crossing later at night. I also wanted to get some idea as to how high the water level might be and if there was a barbed-wire fence.

All the conditions looked very favourable - no barbed wire and also what seemed to be a low water level. I retrieved my rucksack and waited for dusk to set in.

A thick cloud cover and no moonshine made darkness descend quite quickly.

Within a few minutes I reached the river again and in the now rapidly fading light I looked for a spot where the river appeared to be shallow. The river was also much narrower than I had thought when I made my brief exploratory visit during the afternoon and when I found a stretch with stones showing up through the water I knew I had found a suitable spot for my crossing. Apart from the gentle gurgling of the water, all was quiet around me.

I descended from the embankment down to the river and started wading slowly towards the middle of the river when suddenly I found myself targeted by a strong searchlight and was told by a loudspeaker to return immediately to the eastern embankment. With the western embankment only a few metres away should I simply ignore this command and make a dash for it? Back in Rostock I had heard people talking about border guards now being armed and willing to shoot at people attempting to flee to the West.

With that in mind I felt I had no option but to return to the eastern embankment where I was confronted by three very young and indeed armed border guards. One of them shone a torch into my face, presumably in order to establish if I was a juvenile or an adult.

I can feel for you. The despair must have been overwhelming when you were only metres away from reaching your goal.

Standing in front of these three guards I felt completely empty. After all my preparations for this venture and the trials of getting to this place, all I had to show for now was failure.

The guard with the torch ordered me to follow him and we marched back into Creuzburg. We came to a building with lights burning inside that was either the local police station or a detention place run by the border guards. Once inside the building I had to hand over my rucksack and also empty my trouser pockets. Then the guard took me down a dimly lit corridor with what looked like cells on either side. And that is exactly what they were.

As I walked along the corridor with the guard behind me I passed a large cell in which, to my astonishment, were two nuns in their full nuns' habit. I was then put into a cell almost directly opposite them. I found it difficult to imagine that they had had the same misfortune as myself, but for the rest of the night I was too dazed myself to make verbal contact with them across the corridor.

The following morning one guard and a female secretary interrogated me to establish my identity and the reason for my wanting to flee socialist East Germany. Why did I carry those strange drawing and papers on me? Why, if I came from Rostock, had I travelled so far south to escape to the West? How did I come by all the money in my wallet?

I was ill-prepared for all these questions and rather than reveal the plan to visit my father, I changed it to visiting my very frail grandparents just across the border in Breitenbach. In the aftermath of the war, I explained, our relatives had been scattered all over Germany and it was my intention to re-establish contact. I was listened to in obvious disbelief, driven clearly by my inability to explain away the existence of that cartridge with the drawings and papers.

The questioning stopped all of a sudden and I was taken back to another cell where I found a tray with some bread and jam and a jug of coffee. With more daylight now throughout the building I noticed that the two nuns were still in their cell.

Apart from a man in civilian clothing bringing me some food at lunchtime and early in the evening and accompanying me to the WC, I spent the whole day in my cell. It seemed to me that the nuns and myself were the only captives being held.

Early the next morning a uniformed guard appeared to take me to a large room. Behind a long table sat four people, three of them in the now familiar uniform of the border guards but one wore a brown tunic, clearly marking him as a Russian. They all had a sheet of paper in front of them, presumably the notes taken down by the secretary during the interrogation the previous day. I was told to stand in front of the table.

Strangely enough there were no further questions about the mysterious drawings and papers. The three German guards were busily reading the paper in front of them while the Russian merely stared at me.

I was then taken out of the room again but ordered to go in again about ten minutes later.

What was the verdict going to be? All their faces looked quite inscrutable. They started to whisper to each other again and then one of the German guards addressed me.

"We have come to the conclusion," he said, "that you have completely failed to embrace the ideology of our socialist regime. You have shown your contempt by not even joining the FDJ organisation and from what we have heard you carried certain documents on you, whose transfer to the West may have been harmful to the Socialist Government of East Germany. In summary therefore we have decided that you should be sent to a Political Correction Camp for a duration to be decided by the Camp Management but not exceeding three years."

A frightening prospect for a 15-year-old boy.

Thankfully one of the 'judges' allowed me to phone my mother to inform her about my misfortune, where I was being held and the likelihood of not seeing her for quite some time. Despite such terrible news her voice stayed remarkably calm.

I was returned to my cell and noticed that the cell with the two nuns was now empty. That left me as the only captive on this corridor.

Back in Rostock my mother must have sprung into action immediately after our telephone conversation. As I learnt later she immediately went to see Pastor Gallay, who in turn contacted our diocesan bishop in the hope that he might put in a plea for clemency. It was a strange decision by my mother to seek help from an organisation for which our new communist regime had little time.

I never found out if the bishop or his office ever put in a plea for me, but on the morning of the third day I was released, my rucksack was returned to me - empty - and I was told that I could return to Rostock.

A man in civilian clothing turned up and ordered me to follow him. Was it just a trick when I was told I could return to Rostock and was I now really being escorted to what they had described as a political correction camp?

We soon reached a bus stop with a coach standing there marked to go to Eisenach. The civilian asked me to board the coach and he followed immediately behind me. Although we were sitting side by side he never spoke a single word on our short ride to Eisenach.

On arrival we headed straight for the railway station where my strange companion asked for the stationmaster's office. My civilian guard and the stationmaster seemed to know each other and after a short conversation the stationmaster wrote something on a piece of paper and finished it off with an ink stamp. Then he said in my direction: "In eight minutes from platform 2."

Once on the platform my guard gave me the piece of paper the stationmaster had written out and I saw it was a free pass all the way back to Rostock. When I boarded the train, my guard suddenly, with a rather friendly voice, wished me a good journey and even more surprisingly handed me a small envelope with some Ost Marks with the jocular remark that this would keep me from starving on my long journey ahead.

No doubt this money originated from my own wallet which they had seized after my capture.

As the train pulled out of the station towards Erfurt I could hardly believe my good fortune after those traumatic three days.

Still wondering as to what had caused my sudden release I was actually beginning to enjoy my journey home. As we pulled out of our first stop, which was Gotha, I noticed that those two derelict coaches were still standing in the same siding where only a few days earlier I had used them as my overnight shelter. From then on my journey became virtually a mirror image of my initial departure from Rostock except that now I was travelling without having to fear police controls and check-ups. From Magdeburg I telephoned my mother to let her know that that I had been released without any further charges and that I would be back in Rostock that very evening. My mother's sigh of relief was clearly audible on the telephone.

On the last stretch of my journey I cast my mind back again over the events of the last few days. Were we now likely to receive a visit from the Rostock police at our home? Was it possible that they had taken into account that I was still a teenager and that the court session in Creuzburg was merely a lesson to frighten me to the core? Whether it was a cruel hoax or not I shall never know. What it did prove was that the East-West border had indeed become an Iron Curtain.

I received a tremendous welcome back home and not having slept in a bed for over one week, I was looking forward to the comfort of my own bed again. My brothers had taken good care of our hens and rabbits during my absence. Everything seemed to be under control and it was a good feeling to be home again.

The Great Escape

With the Cold War getting colder month by month, West Germany issuing its own constitution and East Germany declaring its own nationhood on 7 October 1949, the earlier post-war hope of the nation's division being only a temporary affair had now finally vanished. If we were to become a reunited family again we had to find a way of getting to Freiburg. After my recent disastrous experience to get there I could not envisage another attempt for an illegal border crossing with my mother and my two younger brothers. The least hazardous escape route would probably still be via Berlin, just as our father had done years before.

With the creation of the German Democratic Republic and the new sense of nationhood, the propaganda for the progressive society was revved up. More political cadres were formed in towns and villages and any open regime-unfriendly behaviour could result in visits from political officials. Attempting to flee the DDR, as it was now commonly referred to, now ranked as a punishable offence.

In this kind of climate, what could we do to prepare our escape? Selling more of our furniture and other belongings would automatically arouse suspicion. My mother had mentioned already that the occupant of the ground floor apartment in the house, who had by now become a full-blooded member of the newly-formed SED, the Socialist Unity Party of Germany and was also the leader of a political cadre, had on several occasions made odd remarks and she was sure that he would report us to the authorities if he became suspicious.

Under these circumstances we decided not to dispose of anything and to continue to portray a sense of complete normality both at school and also with our neighbours and friends at church.

Christmas was a very subdued event. We did not even bother to set up the customary model railway system in our sitting room. Not even the usual carp soup on Christmas Eve. The thought of things to come in the coming year must have lain heavily on all our minds.

In the following weeks I began to collect as much information about the situation in Berlin as I could get. There was a direct railway connection to Berlin but presumably heavily controlled by the police or security guards. One of my trusted school friends mentioned one day that his father, who was a doctor, had been to Berlin to attend a conference. Pretending to be a railway enthusiast I succeeded in getting my friend to tell me a little more about his father's journey. From what I could make out the largest part of the journey was comfortable and trouble-free but on the approach to Berlin at a place called Oranienburg all travellers were subjected to a thorough inspection by the Volkspolizei. That was really valuable information for me and very much influenced the planning of our final escape route.

Meanwhile, however, life continued in as normal a fashion as possible. We started to send small parcels with family papers and mementos, including my stamp collection, to our aunt Trudel in Zwickau.

On 2 April 1950 Pastor Gallay confirmed me into the Lutheran Church, but my mother's plea for help the previous summer was never mentioned. When I looked up the scripture text he had noted down on my confirmation certificate, it crossed my mind that it may have been chosen deliberately in response to my mother's earlier plea.

I managed to give away my beloved rabbits one by one to a few trustworthy school friends and also to the family in our road who - years earlier - had given me my first young rabbits. I was hoping that the Party member in the lower apartment would think that our disappearing rabbits had finally ended up on our kitchen table. Finding a home for our chickens was not so easy, and in the end we decided to just leave them in the hen enclosure but to write a letter to our next-door neighbours from West Prussia to say that they could have them and that we would post that letter from the railway station before leaving Rostock.

In early May we finally filled two suitcases with clothing and a few very personal belongings and over two days I took them one by one on the tram car to the railway station where I deposited them in luggage lockers. Every time on leaving the house I took great care to avoid any encounter with the Party member in the ground-floor apartment. On the morning of the third day we finally closed the door behind us for the very last time and with my mother only carrying a large handbag with some of her remaining jewellery, money and identity papers, the four of us set off for our last tram ride in Rostock.

At the station we retrieved our suitcases and bought our train tickets for Schwerin, the capital of our new state of Mecklenburg-Vorpommern. After I had told my mother about the likelihood of police controls on the fast direct line from Rostock to Berlin we had all agreed that we might be safer by choosing a longer and hopefully less busy route.

Excuse me for interrupting but you describe your departure from your home in a most casual manner. Was it not a great emotional upheaval?

Yes, you are right. It certainly was.

When we finally left our apartment that morning, my mother had tears in her eyes.

For us three boys it did not fully sink in, that we would never come back again and that we would never see again all our treasured toys and memorabilia which had formed part of our lives. Several weighty photo albums had to be left behind and also my naval binoculars, which years before I had found on the abandoned submarine in the harbour and which I had always looked upon as a valued wartime booty. In a way we probably drew some comfort from the fact that so many families had lost everything during the bombing raids on our town and that also our paternal relatives from Silesia had had to leave their homes with probably fewer belongings than what we had in our two suitcases.

My two younger brothers may still have regarded our departure as a new adventure, but I was only too aware of the potential perils, remembering my recent misfortune at Creuzburg. I could also tell that my mother was very fearful of the journey ahead.

Even on the first phase of our journey we received curious looks from our fellow travellers. What was a single woman doing on a train with three boys during school time and two fairly large suitcases above her on the luggage rack?

We really were easy prey for any police inspection or even civilian Party members.

Thankfully the journey to Schwerin was trouble-free. Our plan was to proceed from there to Nauen, a town on the north-western side of Berlin with the intention of switching to local road transport from there on into Berlin.

When looking at the large display board of train arrivals and departures we noticed an almost immediate connection from Schwerin directly to Berlin via Nauen. Should we be bold enough to risk the journey directly into Berlin? A very tempting thought. Could we trust the railway ticket clerk not to give us away when a single woman with three young boys purchased one-way tickets all the way to Berlin?

With the train departure time approaching rapidly we had to make a quick decision. In any case there was always the danger that police controls could occur at any stage of the journey. We decided to stick with the original plan and got our tickets just in time to catch the train.

This time we did not have to suffer the curious stares of other travellers as we had a complete compartment to ourselves. It seemed the train was fairly empty but began to fill up during two stops before reaching Nauen. Thankfully none of the new travellers were policemen or uniformed officials.

By the time the train pulled into Nauen station dusk had descended and we knew that we had to find a shelter for the night. As we walked along the platform I suddenly saw several uniformed men boarding the train and I noticed that their uniforms were identical to the ones worn by the border guards in Creuzburg. What a relief. We had just got off the train in time.

Our two suitcases restricted our movements considerably and since this station did not seem to have any luggage lockers I suggested to my mother that she and my two brothers should stay in the station waiting-room while

I was making enquiries about possible bus routes into Berlin. There was also a HO Imbiss Bar at the station, enabling me to buy some food and drinks for the family. The bus station was just outside the railway station and a well-lit timetable showed several bus routes leading to different parts of Berlin, some of them departing very early in the morning.

Spending a night in a railway station waiting room was nothing new to me but it certainly was a new experience for the rest of the family. Apart from the noise of a few trains passing through the station during the night, all remained peaceful and my brothers seemed to have enjoyed this new experience.

Not really knowing the names of the suburban districts of Berlin we asked one of the bus drivers if the Berlin U-Bahn system stretched as far out into the suburban district that was marked out as the final destination of his bus.

"Sorry," he said, "I am not going that far into Berlin but at my terminal you can get another bus that will take you to several U-Bahn stations."

The way he said all this and judging by the looks he gave us it was fairly obvious that he had a good idea as to why we were asking these questions. It was very likely that we were not the first people to have put such questions to him.

He did not have many passengers on this very early morning trip and our suitcases had ample space at the back of the bus. We soon reached densely urbanised areas and about half an hour later we arrived at the terminal of this bus route with other buses standing there to offer transport further into Berlin. It all looked almost too easy.

It was widely known that the U-Bahn network was still working as a unitary system despite the division of Berlin into four different occupation zones. Our bus had already passed a couple of U-Bahn stations when I said to my mother that we should leave the bus at the next one.

For all of us this was our first encounter with an underground tube system. After lengthy studies of the U-Bahn maps and asking advice from other travellers, we finally worked out how to get to a station called Onkel Toms Hütte, which we knew was nearest to the address of our relatives.

On this journey, good fortune has been very much on your side. Being now on the Berlin U-Bahn must have come as a great relief to you.

To travel all that distance without a single police control and to get off the train at the right time and place really appeared to be a miracle. Having been the planner of this escape route, I did not dare to think of the consequences if things had gone wrong. But here we were, in Berlin, and I felt quite pleased with myself, almost like having achieved another successful border crossing. My mother also looked much more relaxed now and my younger brothers still looked upon it as an exciting adventure.

We knew that our relatives did not have a telephone, which meant we could not even warn them about our imminent arrival. Whilst it may have been relatively easy to give a single person like my father shelter when he arrived many years ago, was their house big enough to offer shelter to a family of four? After all, they were only very distant relations on my father's side and we had not met them before.

After two more changes on the U-Bahn we finally - after a lot of confusion and with the help of other traveller - found the correct line to Onkel Toms Hütte. We also learnt that our destination was in the American sector of the city.

The address in the Zehlendorfer Landstrasse was indeed very close to the U-Bahn station.

When my mother finally pressed the doorbell on what was a small terraced house, I am sure she must have been very apprehensive about the kind of reception we might receive. A middle-aged woman opened the door and it was quite obvious from her facial expression that she thought we were a homeless family going to ask for some food or money. My mother quickly introduced herself and the rather stern face of the woman instantly turned into a warm welcoming smile. We learnt that our relative had in fact been widowed shortly after my father had stayed with them and that she now lived alone in the house.

Before we could even ask for it, we were offered

hospitality for as long as we needed it.

Needless to say we all felt enormously relieved. After shifting a few pieces of furniture we created sleeping facilities for the whole family and after a good clean-up and a meal, during which we told her why and how we had ended up on her doorstep today, we retired to comfortable beds in what was to become our home for the next two months.

The next morning, after posting a letter to our father, I had a look at our new surroundings. Having heard so much about the terrible destruction Berlin had suffered from bombing raids and the fighting at the end of the war I was pleasantly surprised to see that this part of the city had remained completely unharmed.

For my mother and brothers our stay in West Berlin was their first exposure to the free western-style economy. In spite of the widespread destruction in the central sectors of the city, transport facilities were widely available and running smoothly and goods of all kinds were readily available. Our host, however, related to us one day in great detail how the Soviet blockade of the city only a year ago had caused great hardship to the population. Hearing all this made us even more appreciative of our present situation.

At long last we could now also establish direct communications with our father. We were pleased to learn that he had been appointed again to a senior position in the Freiburg Central Post Office and that he had started the process of getting the essential papers for our evacuation from Berlin. A more immediate effect was that we could now receive money transfers from Freiburg.

One morning the postman delivered a large envelope containing the forms on which we had to register our personal details and our status as refugees from the DDR, seeking reunification of our family in West Germany or the German Bundes Republic as it was now called.

It now became a matter of waiting for our applications to be processed.

As the weeks went by, my mother became increasingly concerned not only about the inconvenience we are causing to our host, but also about the fact that none of her boys were receiving any schooling during this unsettled period.

I have to admit that I had quite taken to the general atmosphere of Berlin and very much enjoyed my exploratory trips into the city centre from the nearby U-Bahn station. Reconstruction seemed to be going on at great speed in many parts of the city.

It must have been in early July when we received a letter with precise instructions to report to Gatow Airport, which was the airbase for the British Occupying Forces. When my mother informed our host about the good news, it almost looked as if she was sad to see us go. During our short stay we all had become very fond of her and she had spared no effort to make us feel at home in her small house.

The day of departure finally arrived and as a special bonus my mother decided that we should make the journey to Gatow by taxi. Words alone did not seem enough to thank our host for her kindness and hospitality and my mother parted with one of her remaining pieces of jewellery as a token of our appreciation.

After a lengthy taxi ride through Berlin we finally arrived at the Gatow airbase. The sentry raised the barrier after a few words with the taxi driver and we were driven to a building with a number of civilians standing there already in a queue. There were no other children.

Suddenly a door opened and a soldier told us in German that we should hold our papers ready and follow him inside the building. There were three desks in the reception area, manned by soldiers who checked our paper against a large list in front of them. Without much ado our papers were stamped and we were then led into another room with large windows overlooking the nearby runway.

Way back in Rostock I had seen many a plane taking off from the runways at the Heinkel factories, but now it appeared it was about to become a first personal experience for all of us. A fleeting thought went through my mind that some of those aircraft standing out there may have been the very same ones that had caused so much destruction in Hamburg, Rostock and many other cities only a few years earlier. It felt odd that now these very same aircraft might fly us to a new beginning in the West.

It was not long before another soldier appeared, gesturing us to follow him outside the building where we then walked for quite some distance to a small twin-engined plane.

Our family were asked to board this plane first and with some trepidation we climbed up the short set of steps. After leaving our two suitcases at the back of the plane we were then told to sit down on what looked like long padded benches on either side of the fuselage. Some belts were dangling from the fuselage wall and we were shown how to strap ourselves in.

Never having been on an aircraft before we did not really know what the interior of a passenger plane should look like, but considering our circumstances, I think we and all our fellow passengers were only to happy to be on these benches.

A shudder went through the whole aircraft when the engines were started and we felt the sensation of movement. Unfortunately there were no windows in the part of the fuselage where we were sitting and I could not observe us taxiing out onto the runway. It seemed like a very short run before the small plane actually became airborne.

While in the Gatow waiting room we had already been told that we would be flown to Hannover where we would be taken to a so called 'Transit Camp' for displaced people and refugees from the East. All sort of images went through my mind when I heard the word Transit Camp and I am sure my mother and my brothers were also a little perturbed when the word 'Camp' came up. How long would we be kept there?

Thankfully our worries were groundless. After a flight of only just over one hour we arrived in Hannover and were promptly taken by coach from the airfield to this ominous Transit Camp. It turned out to consist of several rows of what might have been old barracks of the German army or even a prisoner of war camp. A large number of people, including many children, were freely roaming round the place and there certainly was no Camp atmosphere.

Once inside one of the huts I noticed several women and men in white overalls with dust masks hanging round their necks. Suddenly one of the men came towards me and asked me to follow him into one of the narrow cubicles, situated along the wall of the hut. Once inside he covered his face with the dust mask and ordered me to face the wall. Then, without any further explanation he pushed a tube down the back of my shirt and a big cloud of white powder emerged from my short trouser legs and my shirt sleeves.

I had now been de-loused and was now apparently considered fit to enter the German Bundes Republic. After the whole family had gone through the same process and our papers stamped accordingly, we were offered some refreshments and thereafter transport to the Hannover Central railway station. On presentation of our stamped documents we received four free tickets all the way to Freiburg.

Compared with our perilous train and bus journey from Rostock to Berlin only two months earlier, this was now a most leisurely experience. We had a whole compartment to ourselves and the conductor who came to check our tickets was interested in knowing where we had come from and why our final destination was Freiburg. He told us that he himself had been a refugee from Pommerania and he wished us good luck with our new life in Freiburg.

It all seemed almost unreal to me and in a rather strange way I was missing the tensions and uncertainties which had so characterised our travels on the other side of the border.

Life on the Other Side

❀

I would imagine that at this stage you were all starting to wonder what your new life in Freiburg would hold in store for you.

You might find this strange but while there was ample opportunity to discuss such matters amongst ourselves in the privacy of our train compartment, none of us seemed to have enough courage to open the discussion. There were so many questions that we probably did not know where to start and in the end felt more comfortable with not starting a discussion at all.

Meanwhile we watched the countryside rush past our window, becoming hillier as we travelled south and beginning to look quite similar to the landscape on my ill-fated journey to Creuzburg.

In Frankfurt we had to change trains and my mother telephoned our father to give him the details of our arrival in Freiburg. I marvelled at the enormous size of the Frankfurt Central station and the board showing train arrivals and departures to and from so many European destinations. Even our train was shown as going finally to Basel in Switzerland.

When we finally boarded our train we noticed that there would be many fellow travellers and that we would not have the luxury of our own compartment again. And so it was. A middle-aged couple joined us. When they started talking to each other I could hear the odd German word, but most of their communication was not comprehensible. It was only when the gentleman began to read a German newspaper that I ventured to ask him where they were travelling to. It was Basel. With Basel apparently only 60 kilometres from Freiburg, I was beginning to wonder if the people in Freiburg might speak with an equally strong accent.

As we continued our journey south we soon began to see on the eastern side the dark green outlines of what our Swiss fellow travellers explained to us was the Black Forest.

Prior to my previous year's attempt to reach Freiburg, I had already familiarised myself with the names of towns and cities along the Rhine Valley leading up to Freiburg. It gave me quite a buzz when now, sitting comfortably on this train, I actually passed through places like Mannheim, Karlsruhe and Offenburg.

Finally, the train pulled into the Freiburg station and there he was: our father.

We all recognised him immediately and even my brother Dietmar, who had only been a baby when my father had left Rostock seemed to recognise him from the photos my mother had shown him.

The reunion on the station platform had a feeling of unreality. A mixture of emotions - joy and relief. After such a long separation would the family bond together again? Our father had the additional joy of seeing how his baby son Dietmar had developed into a strapping five-year-old.

Did you all have a home to go to?

The answer to that is really yes and no …

Once outside the station our father called a taxi that took us right through the centre to our new domicile in a district called Wiehre.

When the taxi pulled up, the driver seemed reluctant to accept a group of five people and two suitcases, but after a short exchange with my father he allowed us to board his vehicle. It was a relatively short ride but from what I saw I already gained the impression that Freiburg was a large town, probably as large as Rostock.

Although, as I learnt later, Freiburg had also suffered from bombing raids towards the end of the war, the damage was not as severe as those inflicted upon Rostock. Nevertheless housing in Freiburg was also scarce. The shortage was aggravated by the large influx of people from the eastern territories and also now by people like ourselves who had fled from Communist East Germany.

Since arriving in Freiburg our father had rented a small apartment for himself which was unsuitable to accommodate the now-reunited full family. Thankfully, however, he had become friendly with a local family by the name of Riesterer who had a large apartment in a multi-storey residence in the Wiehre district. These people had generously offered to share their apartment with my mother and us three boys until we succeeded in finding a proper family accommodation.

It reminded me of the generous and selfless attitude we had encountered on our arrival in Berlin.

Once again, over a short space of time, we had the good fortune of meeting people who - having themselves been spared the extreme ravages of war - now treated their less fortunate fellow citizens with extraordinary compassion and self-sacrifice. Was it merely an expression of suppressed 'guilt' for having been spared the deprivations of their compatriots?

Already, in my advancing teenage years and even more so in later life, I continued to struggle with the question of how such kind and educated people could possibly be the same ones who only ten or fifteen years earlier had remained silent when terrible atrocities were committed on so many of their fellow Germans. The history books are full of examples of how tyrants and demagogues have turned nations into mindless followers, willing to perform the most heinous deeds, but how could a nation that produced world-renowned artists, inventors, composers and philosophers - plus a strong Christian tradition – have allowed itself to be so easily misled?

You mentioned earlier that the 1919 Treaty of Versailles was regarded as a pure act of vengeance by virtually all levels of German society and that the imposition of harsh, punitive reparations provided the platform for any person with radical views to reach power by even democratic processes.

Yes, my view on this remains unchanged. I think that the general anger may have blinded people's judgements, which then allowed a flawed person like Hitler to reach absolute power within an existing democratic structure. With hindsight one could say that if German academia and also the Church had given greater support to the more moderate streams of German politics, maybe the rapid descent into a brutal dictatorship could have been avoided. We shall never know.

But now, let me come back to our host family in our new home town of Freiburg.

Although conditions were a little cramped, we shared a very happy family life with our hosts and their two teenage sons. To my great relief everybody spoke perfectly clear German albeit with a slightly different intonation and I learnt that Swiss German did not really cross the border at Basel.

At the start of the autumn term I joined the Rotteck Gymnasium, which was classified as a Real Gymnasium in contrast to the Humanistic Gymnasium I had originally attended in Rostock. The new school curriculum put more emphasis on science subjects and being now in the French occupied zone, French became the first compulsory foreign language. On the understanding that I would spend my French lessons with one of the junior beginners classes I was allowed to continue the other subjects with pupils of my own age-group.

I was quite sorry not to be able to continue with Latin in which I had by now reached a good level of competence and which I had also found so helpful in my own attempts to learn Spanish. Understandably Russian lessons did not feature on this school's curriculum.

To my delight I soon discovered that my previous humanistic schooling had provided me with a sufficiently good knowledge of scientific subjects and I found it quite easy to link up with the new curriculum in Freiburg. I soon discovered that several of my new fellow pupils originated from territories east of the river Oder and that their families - like ourselves - had now found refuge in this beautiful capital of the Black Forest.

My new school also provided a very special surprise to a boy coming from the flat lowlands of Mecklenburg. The school apparently owned or hired a large chalet type building on the Schauinsland mountain near Freiburg. My fellow pupils informed me that after the Christmas break the senior classes and their teachers would spend a fortnight at this chalet for their lessons, but more importantly for a lot of skiing. This gave me immediately some clear ideas for my wish list for Christmas. One Saturday afternoon our parents took us into town and at considerable expense, which must have stretched their financial resources, we were kitted out for the winter conditions in this part of Germany.

The two sons of our host family owned several pairs of skis and kindly offered me a pair when they heard about the school outing after Christmas. Trying on ski boots was yet another new experience. These boots with lots of hooks up the front that all had to be laced up were something quite novel to me.

With my brother Lothar also settled in well in his new school and with my father making positive comments about finding a home for the whole family, life began to become almost normal again. We felt more and more like part of the Freiburg community. The huge minster surrounded by a daily colourful market impressed me very much.

Christmas was spent with our remarkable host family with the traditional Christmas Eve meal shared at a huge table by nine people. For my family it was a very historic event as it was our first joint Christmas meal after five years of separation. Long hours were spent telling our father about events back in Rostock, about my failed attempt trying to visit him the previous year, about our escape to Berlin and the airlift to Hannover. This was also our opportunity to hear how our father had reached Berlin and how he had been taken on a French military train from Berlin to West Germany.

When I broached the subject of those drawings and papers that had seemed to be of such interest to my father and that had caused me considerable discomfort after my failed border crossing at Creuzburg, I was very surprised by his explanation.

I had suspected that they may have had something to do with his work during the war. Now I learnt that they were the preparatory drawings and papers for a patent application on a subject completely unrelated to my father's professional background. It had something to do with large multi-axled lorries and possibly also large military road transporters. My father thought he had designed a system for the undercarriage whereby such vehicles could turn on a much reduced radius in relationship to their length. We all knew that our father had always had a wide range of interests but I must admit his interest in heavy road vehicles came as a complete surprise to me.

Time permitting, he said, he would try to recreate those papers - but with the domestic pressures now upon him he never got round to it.

During the Christmas period our hosts alerted us to a small apartment becoming vacant just across the road. Our farther had mentioned before that he was getting increasingly concerned about the health and fitness of our grandparents who at that time still lived in Breitenbach in Hessia. The trauma of their expulsion from their Silesian homeland had obviously left them weak and frail and in need of care. This apartment just across the road would offer an excellent opportunity to bring them closer to us. My father succeeded in securing a lease and in late January my grandparents were safely installed in their new home.

My youngest brother Dietmar had never seen his grandparents before and he looked quite bewildered when he first came face-to-face with my grandfather who was sporting a sizeable but well-groomed moustache. I always thought he looked like Bismarck.

Early in January the day finally came and laden with schoolbooks, personal belongings, warm apparel and above all the pair of skis, we were taken by bus from our school to the lower station of the Schauinsland cable car, just a few kilometres from the city centre. The ride in the cable car cabin was yet another novel experience. Below me was a seemingly endless forest with snow-capped treetops. I was really fascinated by this view and I felt we reached the top station far too quickly. Once there we had to wait for the arrival of several more cabins with teachers and more pupils and also a special cabin with our baggage and the all-important skis.

As I had already feared, all my fellow pupils and also the teachers were clearly experienced skiers. They quickly readied themselves and skied off to the school chalet. I was told it was only half an hour's walk away. Thankfully one of my fellow pupils and our geography teacher took pity on me and walked with me all the way to the chalet with the footpath covered by a thin layer of freshly fallen snow.

The chalet turned out to be an impressive two-storey wooden building with a huge roof reaching almost right down to the ground. Inside it had a warm and welcoming atmosphere and a distinct smell of pine wood. When I saw my room and two rows of comfortable-looking bunk beds, memories of my wartime evacuation to Malchin flashed through my mind. Now, however, there was no early morning assembly and flag hoisting.

As there were no school classes on the settling-in day, my fellow pupils must simply have dumped their baggage in their rooms and returned to the outside slopes where they were showing off their skills. When I saw them racing and elegantly slaloming down those slopes I seriously began to wonder if I would ever reach a similar competence in this sport.

During the ensuing two weeks, attention to the school curriculum suffered badly and skiing - with the silent connivance of our teachers - became the dominant daily activity.

After a few days I was informed that at the end of our fortnight we would not be returning back to Freiburg by cable car but that it was a tradition to make the return journey on our skis. To make things worse I was also told that the early part of the descent was a particularly steep downhill path through the forest, which was locally known as the 'Kalte Wasser' run.

Thankfully two of my fellow pupils, one of whom was a particularly experienced skier by the name of Klaus, took it upon themselves to give me lessons on how to cope with those two long pieces of wood strapped to my feet: how to turn round, how to get up after a fall, how to break one's speed, how to swing into a gentle slalom and how to stop at the end of a downhill run. It was hard work but a wonderful experience.

At the end of the fortnight my two tutors considered me competent enough to master the long downhill run back to Freiburg.

When finally the day of our departure arrived I have to admit I felt very nervous. In a long line, my fellow pupils and our teachers skied effortlessly from the chalet towards the edge of the nearby forest. I joined the end of the line, wondering if the heavy weight of my rucksack would affect me keeping my balance. Klaus kindly volunteered to stay with me, for which I was truly grateful.

The initial stretch was in fact slightly uphill, which I found quite easy, but once we reached the forest the challenge became immediately apparent. In front of us was the Kalte Wasser run, which was really a narrow footpath with trees on either side and with a menacingly steep incline. I realised immediately that on such a narrow path I could not even apply the 'V' formation with my skis to reduce my speed. Furthermore with everyone else having skied down before me the snow had become quite impacted, resulting in even greater speed. How I wished we could all have gone back home by cable car.

With an encouraging final nod from Klaus I pushed myself forward into the downward run. To this day I still do not know how I managed to stay on my feet.

With trees flying past me at ever-increasing speed, the whole ordeal lasted only about six minutes but at the time it seemed an eternity. At the end the run filtered out into a gentle sloping meadow, covered in nice powdery snow, furrowed by lines left behind by the skis of my fellow pupils who had gone before me.

As I slowed down I suddenly had a strange sensation in my legs, a feeling as if they were going to buckle under me. Meanwhile my tutor friend Klaus had also arrived, looking very relaxed. He admitted that he had done this popular run several times before. He congratulated me on my performance and we jointly proceeded with our descent to Freiburg.

Judging by your enthusiastic description of your first sojourn into the wintery mountains of the Black Forest and even becoming a skier, did this make you feel that Freiburg had really become the town you now called your own?

I have to admit that since arriving in Freiburg I often thought back to our days in Rostock. I had always been very fond of the sea, the sandy beaches at Warnemünde with their colourful array of canopied beach chairs, the fishing boats unloading their catches at the narrow harbour front, noisy seagulls swooping down to feast on anything that fell overboard and the invigorating, salty breezes wafting in from the Baltic Sea. These memories, I hope, will always stay with me in the same way as I try not to forget many other episodes and events during my sometimes turbulent formative years.

Back in Freiburg my family and our hosts seemed to be very pleased to see me come home without any broken bones or injuries. When I returned the loaned skis to our host's son Helmut, he admitted he was astonished that I had managed the Kalte Wasser run, which he knew from his own experience to be a challenging one. I felt very pleased with my 'baptism of downhill skiing' and I was sure that it would help me significantly with my own personal standing amongst my fellow Gymnasiasts, to whom I was still the newcomer from the flat lowlands of the north. It also led to a lifelong friendship with my skiing tutor Klaus.

In the summer our parents finally secured an apartment in the Merzhauser Strasse and the whole family was under one roof again.

With all the attractions our new home town had to offer and our father's finances only permitting what we regarded as inadequate pocket-money, my brothers and I were soon looking for ways to supplement our allowances. Not far from our new home were the large Vauban Barracks, the quarters of the French occupational force. Somehow we must have heard from somebody that the chefs of the army canteen paid generously for freshly collected snails of a variety found in the vineyards around Freiburg. To our delight we found this to be absolutely true and by scouring the nearby vineyards once or twice per week our financial position improved significantly.

With our increased involvement in Freiburg's cultural and social life, curiosity drove me one evening to attend a meeting at the university, organised by the European Youth Movement. Most of the attendees were university students but there were also representatives of political parties, members of the Freiburg Civic Council and a number of teenagers of my own age group.

It soon became apparent that several of the speakers had gone through war- and post-war experiences probably similar to ours and that these people here in this university hall were - like me - seeking answers to so many questions which had remained unanswered by our elders. And here now they had come together to air their own views on how this war-ravaged continent might rise from its ashes again.

I felt captivated by the debate and at the close of the evening I asked one of the student organisers to formally enlist me as a member of the European Youth Movement.

Sorry, but did you not have enough of politics from your earlier pre- and post-war years?

Yes, I probably had - but this now seemed different. Here were young people grappling with ideas and visions for a peaceful coexistence among the former warring nations and having endured the indoctrinations by two totalitarian administrations in my earlier years, I felt truly drawn to this new movement of free thinkers and enthusiasts.

I began to attend meetings regularly and readily volunteered to distribute leaflets to my fellow pupils, to university students - in fact to anyone who looked in their late teens or early twenties.

At one of our meetings we had the Chancellor Konrad Adenauer as our guest speaker and we felt very honoured that he had found the time to visit us in this remote southern corner of Germany. It soon became clear that Freiburg had a very personal pull for him as he had been a student at the university.

During the summer school holiday, instead of making perilous journeys across the Iron Curtain, I now joined bus trips to meetings with members of the European Youth Movement in France and towards the end of the summer break we even travelled as far as Mallorca, which gave me a chance to try out my self-taught Spanish.

My membership of this growing youth movement certainly stirred up my general interest in political developments not only in Germany, both East and West, but in the growing reconciliation between Germany and our neighbour France with the border just a few kilometres west from Freiburg.

It brought back memories of my days on the farm in Broock, where Louis as a prisoner of war and I as a child evacuee had shared many happy hours together. Way back, Louis once mentioned that his home town was Mülhausen in Alsace, but since I didn't know his family name, I did not see a chance of tracing him again, which I would have dearly loved to do.

At our regular meetings we followed with interest the

proposals by the French politician Robert Schuman about economic and industrial collaboration and learnt that his ideas were readily shared not only by Germany but also by a number of other European nations.

Are you referring to what became known as the Coal and Steel Community?

Yes, I am amazed you actually remember this treaty which, as you know, became the building block for a much more embracing association of nation states as later encapsulated in the Treaty of Rome.

With tensions between East and West visibly growing month by month, it filled us with great comfort that the people on this side of the Iron Curtain showed undiminished resolve to put old grievances aside. The growing awareness of the oppressive conditions on the other side of the Iron Curtain no doubt helped the western nations to bury old entrenched prejudices and to value even more the freedom available to them in this post-war era. Having spent virtually all my formative years under totalitarian regimes, I found this form of unfettered freedom very stimulating and thought-provoking.

It filled me therefore with dismay and even anger when several years later our youthful vision of a family of European nations was hijacked by politicians who pursued what seemed to become a power-grabbing agenda with an arrogant disregard for the cultural and historic values cherished by the members of this new club of West

European nations. As years went by it struck me more and more that the emerging powerhouse mentality, displayed by unelected apparatchiks began to show similarity with the oppressive and dictatorial administrations I had lived through in the past. Surely, two dictatorships in a person's lifetime was more than enough.

Sorry that I have been going on about this topic at some length but as you will have noticed it is a matter about which I have strong feelings. Now, let me get back to the main strand of my recollections.

Well, I am very grateful that you expressed yourself so passionately on this important topic.

For me the time had also come to make up my mind as to what kind of career to take up. Should I stay on at the Rotteck Gymnasium to complete my academic education or should I seek my future in the world of industry and commerce?

With German industry beginning to show signs of rapid recovery, widely referred to as the 'Wirtschaftswunder'or Economic Miracle I began to think that I would quite like to be part of this revival.

After my final exams at the Rotteck Gymnasium in 1952 I signed up with the Higher Commercial College in the district of Haslach in Freiburg for an intensive one-year course. Now, apart from economics, company management, book-keeping and a host of related subjects, I had also my first introduction to the English language, albeit only one lesson per week. The college, however, had to offer another novel experience. For the first time in my life I shared a classroom with female students. It was also the year in which I struck up a lasting friendship with Gert.

Most of my fellow students were the sons or daughters of business owners in the Freiburg region who, on completion of the college course, would obviously join their family businesses. At the recommendation of one of our tutors I submitted an application to a well-known local textile company by the name of Mez AG, who were one of the leading suppliers of sewing threads for domestic and industrial uses in Germany. I received a very prompt invitation for an interview and was accepted for a two-year apprenticeship. I started work immediately and for the next two years was put through a rigorous training programme not only in the administrative offices but also in the factories and dye houses. I also used the period of my apprenticeship to take driving lessons and eventually, with a licence in my pocket, I began to feel quite 'adult'.

My final exam results must have given my employer sufficient confidence to appoint me soon afterwards as manager of their regional warehouse in Munich.

Once again I set off on a train journey into the unknown, with plenty of advice from my parents who were clearly pleased to see me taking my first step on my career ladder. My arrival at the Munich Central station reminded me of our stop-over in Frankfurt in 1950. This was another enormous domed station with platforms as far as the eye could see.

When I showed my piece of paper with the address of my prearranged accommodation to the taxi driver, I realised that once again I was confronted with another version of the German language. He quickly noticed my discomfort and repeated in clear language that my destination was virtually round the corner from the station but that he would take me there. My new abode was a small 'pension' in the Schwanthaler Strasse and the owner was a middle-aged lady who, judging by her language, had not originated from this part of the country. I was shown a small but comfortable room on the fifth floor of the building with a rather uninspiring view over the backyards of other houses.

With the help of a street map I quickly established the whereabouts of the Mez warehouse and driven by curiosity and also to establish the walking time to get there, I decided on a prompt visit. It was a leisurely walk of only about 15 minutes but when I finally got there I felt rather disappointed. I had expected a smart building with a wide entrance and possibly large lettering on its frontage to signify to the public that this was a distribution centre of Mez AG. Instead I was confronted with what may have been a burnt-out building made usable again after the war but still looking like a ruin, with the name of the company on a small plastic board above the entrance.

I returned back to my 'pension' rather disappointed and began to wonder what the following day would bring when starting my role as manager of this place.

When I arrived the regional sales representative and three warehouse staff gave me a warm welcome. Rows and rows of shelves with our products gave an instant impression that in spite of its exterior appearance, this was a distribution centre dealing with a significant volume of business. I began to look forward to my role as manager.

It was only a week or so after I had stared work that a customer said to me: "you know, of course, that Mez is a Scottish company?" I replied that I was not familiar with the ownership situation of the company.

This comment however awakened a question I had asked myself during my apprenticeship in Freiburg. One of the departmental managers was a gentleman from Scotland who was also a member of the company's board. Now the presence of this gentleman in Freiburg began to make sense.

I really began to enjoy living in a city so rich in culture and history and earning a respectable salary. Having become familiar with the tram network I decided to seek some larger accommodation on the outskirts of the city.

After a short search I found a place in the Rosenheimer Strasse on the outskirts of Munich. Virtually outside the house was the terminal tram stop of the line that took me straight to my work and the beginning of the autobahn to Salzburg was only a few hundred metres away.

Once again I was lucky not only to find comfortable accommodation but also to be received with an instant expression of friendliness and hospitality. I soon learnt that my elderly landlord couple had lost their two sons during the final phases of the war and were clearly pleased to have the company of a young man again.

In the apartment above lived the Koch family. Their son Walter was of my own age. He worked for the Bavarian Radio Station but also played an active part in the Munich Film Studios. Born and bred in Munich and being deeply involved in the social scene in the city, he introduced me to a wide variety of cultural and folkloric events and also to yet another sporting activity: ice skating.

Having made good progress in mastering the local language, enjoying my new managerial role at the warehouse and now also leading a varied and exciting social life, I have to admit that I became fonder of this city and its people day by day. A visit to the famous October Beer Festival left me in no doubt that this city could also be a noisy and even raucous place but it still fitted with the general sentiment of 'joi de vivre' which seemed to prevail. I did not miss the opportunity of downing many a jug of the delicious local beer myself.

Listening to you one gets the impression that you have drawn a line under the past and instead have thrown yourself into a completely new lifestyle. Politics suddenly seemed to have disappeared from your agenda.

You are absolutely right. Bonn had become a far-away place, the local newspapers were full of local news and being now part of the business world my interest in the European Project began to fade a little. Also I found it very difficult to resist the multitude of attractions Munich and its surroundings had to offer.

One such attraction was the ski slopes in the nearby Alps. Although I still considered myself a skiing novice I signed up for a weekend excursion to the resort of Kufstein in Austria. Soon after our arrival it became obvious that all my fellow travellers were seasoned skiers, but not wishing to display my own meagre experience I also took the ski lift up to the top of the slope and mastered a few downhill runs with in-between stops.

When the time of departure came a group of us decided to take a short cut back to the coach through a small forest. When we reached the edge of the wood it reminded me of my memorable 'baptism of skiing' in the Black Forest. I followed one of the lead skiers, feeling quite confident, when suddenly my right ski went underneath a snow-covered fallen tree trunk and my left ski went over it.

The outcome of all this was a broken leg, which thankfully did not cause me too much pain. My fellow travellers helped me back to the coach and after being given a double seat on which to rest my raised leg, we travelled back to Munich. After discharging my fellow travellers in the centre of Munich the coach driver volunteered to take me to the nearest hospital where I received very prompt attention. The X-ray confirmed a clean break of my shin bone and I ended up with a solid plaster all the way up to my thigh - and a strong walking stick.

With instructions to report to my nearest local doctor I was released that very same evening and a taxi took me back to my abode in the Rosenheimer Strasse with one surplus skiing boot in my rucksack.

The hospital staff had already assured me that if I had an office job and the opportunity to rest my leg that there was no reason to be bedbound. With that sort of encouragement I decided to make the usual tram journey to my office on Monday morning and was very grateful for helping hands to get me up and down the steep steps of the Munich tram cars.

I hobbled around with my plaster leg for over one month, but having been told that it was a clean break I felt at least confident that this episode would not leave me with any long-lasting problems.

With both legs operational again - but still advised not to take up ice skating for another month or so, - I was pleased when Walter suggested one weekend that we should visit Salzburg, travelling there by air and back by train.

Having had the experience of our air lift from Berlin to Hannover in a military plane, this would now show me what the interior of a civilian plane looked like.

The airport at Riem itself was a new experience. Large halls, shops and departure-and-arrival boards created the atmosphere of an international hub of activity, very different from the utilitarian military ambience of the Gatow air base in Berlin.

The twin-engined plane looked even smaller than the one in Berlin, but now we had soft seats with adjustable backs and above all we had windows that allowed us to marvel at the Alpine mountain range and its snow-capped peaks. The flight came to an end all too soon.

After some rather hasty sightseeing in Salzburg, an early evening train took us back to Munich and concluded an exciting day out.

The approaching Christmas season transformed the city into a bewildering profusion of lights and decorations. Window dressers must have let their imagination run wild with the often humorous and imaginative window displays in the major shops. It was also time to decide on my travel plans for visiting the family back home in Freiburg. Since I had to be back in Munich for the year-end inventory at the warehouse, I travelled on a very early train on Christmas Eve with my return ticket already booked for three days later.

Our mother had done her best to create the atmosphere of Christmasses of the years gone by, the beautifully decorated Christmas tree, her home-baked stollen cake and a delicious goose for the Christmas dinner table, but somehow the excitement we had experienced in our younger days was no longer there.

Freiburg itself had put on a very festive appearance and the bells of the minster added majestically to pronouncing the Christmas message.

With only a few days at my disposal, visits to friends and also our recently widowed grandfather had to be kept short and although the snow conditions were ideal I even had to turn down a suggestion by my father to try again some gentle skiing on the Schauinsland mountain. May be it was really the fear of another accident and a re-fracture of my right leg that made me decline this offer.

On the day of my departure the whole family saw me off at the station and I remember that just before boarding the train my father said to me: "Be careful not to let that Bavarian accent dominate your way of speaking. You do not know yet where your future career will take you and I think good High German will get you further".

Here was a clear paternal parting shot. It reminded me that - even in Rostock - our father had never used the widely spoken Low German and was clearly a great believer in the purity of our language. It also brought home to me that during my relatively short time in Munich I had definitely acquired a clearly recognisable Bavarian accent.

Back in Munich and with the end-of-year inventory concluded, New Year celebrations quickly saw me immersing myself again into the social scene of Walter and his friends.

One gets the impression that you felt more at home in Munich than Freiburg.

To be honest, you are right. It struck me even more so

when - in the spring of 1956 - I received instructions from my employer to return to Freiburg by the middle of the year. Although the recall implied some personal career advancement I felt really unhappy having to leave this exciting city and the circle of friends I had built up during my stay here.

My deep affection for this vibrant city never really left me and when many years later I tried to give my future Scottish wife an insight into life in Germany, I chose Munich as our destination.

After several rounds of lively farewell parties I returned to Freiburg where I learnt about my promotion to sales clerk in the Industrial Sales department.

My new status was underpinned by a shared secretary, which was a major step up in my career progression. Strangely enough, my office was almost next door to the one occupied by that mysterious gentleman from Scotland whose role I now began to see more clearly

It did not take long to re-establish myself, but I have to admit that compared with Munich, life in Freiburg was clearly running at a lower gear. I quickly rejoined my old circle of friends from the Gymnasium, the Commercial college and also the European Youth Movement. For reasons I simply cannot remember I even enrolled at the university for a basic course in nuclear physics designed for members of the general public.

The one person missing in all this was my old friend Klaus, who had given me my first skiing lessons at the school chalet. I visited his parents in the outlying district of Guenterstal and learnt that Klaus, now working for the Deutsche Bank, had asked for a transfer to Berlin. It became clear very quickly that Klaus's father was not pleased with this relocation, because he himself had been a professional soldier and did not approve of Klaus choosing to 'escape' to Berlin, where young men of our age group were exempt from conscription into the newly formed German army. We were generally referred to as the 'White Age Group' and - from what I heard - very few of us ever got the dreaded call-up letter. Klaus clearly did not want to take that risk and his employer readily found him a position in one of their Berlin branches. It was only years later that we joined up again in Freiburg.

Being the proud owner of a driving licence I was determined to use my annual leave for some exploratory trips round Germany or the neighbouring countries. I approached my other close school friend, Gert, who readily agreed to take his annual leave at the same time as mine, and to hire a motorcycle. Gert's paternal family originated from Alsace and he suggested that we do a tour of France with the prime destination being Paris, where he had a cousin who worked in a fashion house. His proposal sounded very appealing.

The choice of rentable motorcycles appeared to be somewhat limited, as I felt insufficiently confident to handle some of the heavier BMW models on offer. In the end we settled for a 125cc Wanderer. It turned out to be a very reliable machine and even with the weight of two riders and our baggage, the relatively small engine worked wonders. As all this was meant to be a low-cost mystery tour with no fixed destination except Paris, we also hired a small tent, which - folded up - neatly fitted into Gert's rucksack.

My initial suggestion was that we cross the border and the river Rhine at nearby Breisach with a leisurely trip through Alsace, the region I automatically associated with the French farmhand Louis who had taught me so many things about animals and life on a farm when I was an evacuee boy in Broock. Gert, however, suggested that we route ourselves via Strassburg where he had an aunt and where, he said, a good meal could always be expected and possibly even an envelope with a few French Francs in it.

Although Strassburg had looked so near on the map, it took us hours to get to the border crossing at Kehl. It was at this stage that I was beginning to wonder if our annual leave of 14 days would actually be long enough to visit the most western regions of the country as we both seemed to be quite keen to see the English Channel. On top of all this, with Gert not having a driving licence, I was the only driver throughout this tour.

However, here we were - with Strassburg begging us on the other side of the Rhine - and so I put my worries aside.

Gert's aunt, who lived in a very spacious apartment, was overjoyed to see us in spite of this being a completely unannounced visit. We were offered accommodation for the night and as Gert had already indicated, the evening was concluded with a delicious meal and with Gert bringing his aunt up-to-date on family matters back in Freiburg. In the morning Gert's other prediction also turned out to be correct: on bidding us farewell the aunt handed Gert an envelope, the contents of which covered our financial needs for nearly a week.

After a quick sightseeing trip through Strassburg, which to my astonishment was full of picturesque canals and waterways, we headed west towards the ancient town of Metz. We both thought that this town was worth a visit as it was a place which had become symbolic for the old rivalries between France and Germany.

It was a glorious day and driving along without any haste we very much enjoyed the ever-changing landscape of the Lorraine region. We deliberately avoided the major roads, so our route took us through picturesque little villages where Gert could show off his superior French whenever we stopped for refreshments or a meal.

In the late afternoon, on our approach to Metz, we found ourselves on a quiet straight road. I thought that this would be the right time and location to suggest to Gert that he might like to have a try at driving our motorcycle. After all, on these quiet country roads the likelihood of a police patrol was very remote.

Gert was only too pleased to have a go and after a few minutes of instructions and a promise not to go beyond first gear he confidently completed a short distance with me running beside him. I suggested that over the next few days we repeat this exercise in suitable locations to achieve a level of competence where he could use the vehicle in an emergency, albeit without an official licence.

After Gert's successful initiation into the basic skills of driving our motorcycle we decided to test our skills further by setting up our small tent. Surrounded by fields and hedgerows we had no problems in finding a suitable place just off the road. A signpost we had passed earlier had indicated that we were 15 kilometres away from Metz.

When Gert unfolded the tent canvas we discovered to our dismay that there was no groundsheet. Some dry grass and an arm full of twigs from a nearby little spinney provided a natural groundsheet on this very first night but at the next opportunity a proper cotton sheet had to be purchased.

With his bundle of aluminium tubes, Gert managed to put up the tent very quickly. It turned out to be roomier than I had expected and quite cosy. Our motorcycle was left close to the front end of our tent and since we had not brought a chain and lock I resorted to a simple method of protection I had once read about in a children's book. I tied one end of a piece of fine string to the front wheel and the other end inside the tent to my left foot. Apart from the occasional noise of a passing car on the nearby road we had a peaceful night and felt quite reassured that our little tent would provide us with comfort and shelter for the rest of our tour.

The following morning we set off for the final few kilometres to Metz with a short stop in a roadside village where the local baker's shop offered the most delicious freshly baked croissants.

Soon afterwards we saw the skyline of Metz, dominated by what appeared to be a very large cathedral. After crossing a river which we learnt later merged with the river Moselle in Metz, we soon reached the outer suburbs of what turned out to be a very picturesque city, bustling with life and full of historic landmarks. A restaurant owner kindly allowed us to leave our motorcycle and baggage safely in his back yard, which gave us the opportunity to explore this astonishing place on foot. The city had clearly escaped the ravages of the last war and the imposing vestiges of German architecture dating back to the late eighteenth and early nineteenth century were easily recognisable. Shady narrow streets were filled with shops of all descriptions and it did not take us long to find one where we bought a quilted groundsheet and another nearby where we bought a chain and lock for the bike.

A brief visit to the imposing cathedral was followed by walking around the numerous squares and the arcades at the Place Saint Louis. After lunch at the Kerstmarkten and having decided on Verdun as our next destination, we returned to the friendly restaurant owner to retrieve our motorcycle. We both felt we could easily have spent another day in this interesting and beautiful city, which I remember Gert aptly describing as a melting-pot of two great central European cultures.

Road signs mentioning Reims proofed to be a great help in guiding us through the suburbs in the right direction for Verdun, our agreed target for the day.

Verdun was only about 90 kilometres away and without haste - and stopping in a small village to buy some food for our evening meal - we eventually reached the outskirts. On our approach we noticed the wide stretches of meadows on both sides of the road covered in rows of undulating low hills, almost like oversized mole hills.

I presume you were both fully aware of the tragic role this location had played in 1916 and the atrocious casualties suffered by the French and German armies.

Yes, our school history books had covered this episode in great detail and when we saw for ourselves the cemeteries stretching out to the horizon one cannot escape the fundamental question: how was it possible that only 25 years later these two nations were at each other's throat again?

After crossing the river Meuse we passed the impressive but also sombre-looking Verdun War Memorial fronted by endless rows of crosses. I thought to myself at the time that all politicians or rulers set upon solving disputes by military means should be made to come here first to let them see the woeful tide of death and destruction which their flippant signing of a declaration of war can cause.

Being here now suddenly made me quite proud of my involvement in the European Youth Movement and being part of finding a new vision for our war-ravaged continent.

On the outskirts of the town we found an inviting little place on the edge of a small forest to pitch up our tent. The new quilted groundsheet was pure luxury.

The field in front of our tent also had a number of those little hills we had earlier noticed on our approach to Verdun and one could not help feeling that all the ground underneath our feet around here had once been the scene of death and anguish. In a leaflet we picked up the next day we learnt that in this bloodiest and longest of all the WWI battles, nearly 800,000 French and German soldiers lost their lives or were wounded. No wonder the soil underfoot felt like ground drenched in blood.

It was an eerie kind of night. After our meal Gert wanted to discuss our target for the next day's travelling, but I felt so tired that I suggested we leave that for the next morning. With the motorcycle securely tied up with our new chain and lock, I did not need to resort to the extra protection with my piece of string. Our new groundsheet contributed greatly to a good night's sleep. In fact we slept so well that we remained completely unaware of some night-time visitors. When I awoke I noticed some additional brightness in the tent. And then I saw it. Right behind my makeshift headrest the tent canvas showed a hole the size of a fist with very frayed edges. I suggested that the culprit may have been a rabbit but Gert was sure that the frayed edges meant we had been visited by rats.

After our breakfast we spread out our map of France to decide on the general direction of our onward journey westwards. I was quite keen to visit Calais, which I had heard was the main crossing-over point for rail, road and passenger traffic to England, but Gert suggested that we tour the more picturesque region further south with places like Honfleur or the elegant coastal site of Deauville, which he explained was not very far from the beaches where the Allied forces had landed in June 1944. At least we were both agreed that we wanted to reach the Channel and with merely ten days left of our annual leave and Paris still our prime target, it became clear very quickly that we would have to cover at least 150 km per day on our 125cc Wanderer motorcycle. It also became clear that whatever coastal destination we would finally choose, time for leisurely sightseeing as we had enjoyed in Metz would become more limited. I did not wish to scare Gert too much at this stage but I knew that some illegal driving by him would also become unavoidable. Although the distance to Honfleur and Deauville was longer than to Calais, Gert was very persuasive and in the end I accepted his plan. In return, I thought this was the right moment to threaten him with the prospect of having to do some illegal driving. He took it quite calmly.

Having originally set out on this 'French Odyssey' without any fixed destination except Paris, we now had an agreed plan and we gave ourselves three days to reach the Channel coast, always hoping that our little 125cc engine would not let us down.

The map told us that we should be heading in the direction of Soisson, which was nearly 200 kilometres away, but with the map showing long stretches of thinly populated countryside I thought that this offered an opportunity to let Gert gain more confidence with driving our motorcycle.

Soon after leaving the Verdun area and passing two more war cemeteries we found ourselves on a straight long road, ideal for a driving lesson. I have to admit that with Gert now sitting in front of me and me giving him instructions over his shoulder I felt a little squeamish for the first few minutes, but once we got into top gear and Gert began to hum a tune, I soon relaxed.

It was obvious that Gert quickly began to enjoy this new experience. Eventually, when we saw a small village in front of us, we changed seats again just in case a local gendarme crossed our path.

It was a friendly-looking village that not only had a bakery shop with an astonishing variety of breads, rolls and cakes but also a petrol station to fill up the near-empty tank and also to pump up the increasingly flat-looking tyres. All these transactions Gert performed in what sounded to me like flawless French.

With me back in the driving seat and a short stop for lunch we covered a good distance, but soon had to admit that Soisson - our target for the day - was a place too far.

When passing through a stretch of woodland we noticed a lay-by with rough benches and tables, probably a place where at weekends people came for walks in the forest and for picnics. To our surprise there was also a small hut which looked like a water closet. An ideal place to pitch up for the night. Gert soon found a good place to set up our tent and unlike on previous nights we had our evening meal sitting comfortably at a table. For extra security the motorcycle was chained to a tree trunk. During our meal several motor cars passed by on the adjacent road but nobody stopped to make use of this very inviting facility.

As you are now moving westwards into a part of France which had suffered badly in 1940 but then also had to endure so much devastation during the period of liberation in 1944, did you feel that people gave you the cold shoulder when they realised from your numberplate on your motorcycle that you were from Germany?

Our contact with the local population was basically restricted to buying food and petrol, where we encountered politeness and often also praise for having chosen France as our destination for our annual holiday. There were, however, also a few occasions when Gert - asking local people for help in finding the right direction - was either completely ignored or received some response with words which, so he said, are not normally found in a dictionary.

But I can fully understand the reason for your question.

After all, we were now moving towards the hinterland of the D-day invasion in 1944 in which so many towns and villages had suffered terrible devastation, not only through on-the-ground fighting but also through massive aerial bombardments. And yet here we were in this picturesque Picardy region, the scene of suffering in not just one but two world wars, admiring the landscape and the homely-looking villages and enjoying the delicious offerings in the boulangeries. It was quite hard not to stop whenever we passed one of these shops.

As we tried to cover a good distance that day, we decided to bypass Soisson and head in the direction of a town called Vernon which we hoped would then leave us with just another day's travel to the Channel coast.

Travelling southwards from Soisson we soon reached the Foret de Compiègne, well-known from our history lessons as the place where the armistices between the warring powers were signed in 1918 and also in 1940. Somewhere I had read that the two original railway coaches in which the signing had taken place were no longer there as the German Government had moved them to Germany in 1944, for fear that they might be used again for the signing of yet another armistice. Apparently the two original coaches were destroyed during the final days of the war.

With the images of wartime cinema newsreels and newspaper pictures still lingering in my memory, I had almost expected to drive into burnt-out villages the further west we travelled, but instead the roads were excellent and the houses, shops, public buildings and churches all looked as if nothing had ever happened to them. However, 12 years had passed since then and clearly the French did not waste any time in rebuilding their homeland. It all gave the strong impression that the much talked about 'Wirtschaftswunder' was not just confined to West Germany but was also actively embraced by our neighbour, France. Maybe the now passionately promoted rapprochement at the highest political level had provided the foundation for both nations to prosper again and to speed up the healing process.

With those thoughts going through my mind again I suddenly felt quite proud to have played my small part in the early days of the European Youth Movement.

With Gert volunteering again to do a stretch of illegal driving we finally reached the coastal region and agreed to head for Deauville, which - according to Gert - was a very elegant resort and a favoured holiday destination for people from Paris. Also he said the beach there was not marred by remnants of German wartime fortifications as was the case further down the Normandy coast. Personally, I would have quite liked to have a look at these remnants of what had become known as the West Wall because in 1940 my Uncle Walter must have travelled up and down this very same coastline to carry out his land surveying job for the German authorities. As I mentioned earlier, this did not save him from eventually being sent to the Eastern front and enduring years of captivity.

As we reached the outskirts of Deauville I noticed the large number of hotels and guest houses, beautifully kept gardens and lots of road signs pointing in the direction of what were clearly the main attractions in this resort. Amongst them featured predominantly the sign pointing towards 'La Plage'. It was at his stage that I began to wonder if in this fashionable and clearly very prosperous place we would find a quiet secluded corner for pitching up our tent for the night. Maybe among the dunes on the beach?

Soon afterwards we reached the seafront and in front of us was an enormous expanse of flat sandy beach with rows of colourful beach umbrellas. It became immediately clear that this was not camping territory.

With our financial resources still looking quite healthy, Gert suggested that we consider one of the guest houses we had noticed on our way into Deauville but finally we decided - with still an hour or so of daylight available - to head north on the coastal road in the hope of finding a more countrified place for the night.

Strangely, after only a short ride, we found ourselves in yet another elegant seaside resort called Trouville but shortly afterwards we found some shrubland for our overnight stay.

I could not help telling Gert that evening that while I had found the enormous expanse of the Deauville beach impressive, the white sands and the dunes of the beaches where I came from could easily hold their own. They were much more intimate beaches, as they were only exposed to minimal tidal movements.

"I hear what you say," said Gert. "The big difference is that your beach is behind a menacing Iron Curtain and Deauville is readily accessible."

Before we closed down for the night it became quite clear that Gert wanted to have a closer look at Deauville before we started our return journey towards Paris.

The next morning we packed up our few belongings and shortly after sunrise headed back to Trouville and then past the very crowded marina of Deauville back to the coastal road along La Plage in Deauville itself. Gert suddenly nudged me in the back and told me to have a look at the beach. Way out, I saw two horses trotting at considerable speed and pulling what looked like a very flimsy two-wheeled carriage. Gert, who had clearly done some homework on Deauville, explained that horse-racing at the local Hippodrome was one of the main features of Deauville and that if we had had more time he would have quite liked to go to a meeting. It was a sport I had never paid much attention to, but what I had seen in films and magazines had always given me the impression that visitors turned up properly and elegantly attired. Gert admitted that in our state of dress he would not have got past the entry gate.

After breakfast in a lively little café we headed for a Post

Office where Gert telephoned his cousin in Paris to let her know that we would be arriving the following day. She informed Gert that she would be booking two rooms for us in the students' residence of the Paris University in the Avenue de la République in the 11th Arrondisement. The keys could be collected from the bursar's office on site but we had to make sure to get there before 7pm.

After a more detailed study of our increasingly shabby roadmap, we concluded that Paris was about 200 kilometres away and taking into account that we would need some time in actually finding the university, we both felt that with an early morning start we could complete our journey the following day before 7pm. Gert, clearly very keen to see more of Deauville, suggested we take a leisurely ride through the resort and at least drive past the landmarks like the Casino building and the Hippodrome.

We even treated ourselves to a proper lunch in an open-air restaurant at the southern end of the beach with a magnificent view onto the open sea. Little did I know at this stage that the land across the sea would one day have a decisive influence on my whole personal future. However, that was another border still to cross.

Near the restaurant we also found a public carpark where we could leave our motorcycle and could access the beach, away from the Promenade and the rows of beach umbrellas. Early in the morning on our return to Deauville I had again been struck by the enormous expanse of the main beach. Now, as we settled down for a little siesta and some sun-bathing, I noticed that the beach had shrunk drastically, demonstrating very visibly the effect of the strong tidal movements on this coastline.

After another ride through Deauville, refuelling and buying some postcards, we decided to search for a camping site south of Deauville. It was only a few kilometres outside the resort that we saw a small piece of grassland next to what looked like a drainage ditch, which appeared ideal for our overnight stay.

Furthermore, the road we had just travelled on seemed to be a very convenient connection to the route we had selected to get to Paris the following day.

Gert quickly pitched up our little tent and as we wanted to make an early start in the morning we settled down quite early. The traffic on the adjacent road remained busy throughout the evening, which prompted me to resort again to my extra safety device for our motorcycle - connecting the front wheel of the motorcycle to my left foot by a piece of thin thread.

In spite of the almost continuous traffic on the road we had a very restful night. Having camped virtually on the edge of a water-filled ditch it had crossed my mind that we might have some nightly visitors again, as had happened near Verdun, but in the morning we still had only one hole in our tent wall.

With the very efficient French way of marking roads and towns we soon found the road to Lisieux, passing through very thinly populated farmland and only one small hamlet, where a garden nursery and seed merchant thankfully also had a small cafeteria where we stopped for breakfast. Bearing in mind that we had to reach our Paris destination before 7pm we decided not to visit Lisieux but to continue our journey on the Route National 13 to Evreux. I would have liked Gert to do another stretch of illegal driving, but since this Route National was a very busy highway and probably also more exposed to police patrols I concluded that for this whole long trip to Paris I had to be the driver.

On our journey so far we had always tried to avoid the major highways. The one we were on now was obviously one of the main roads leading in and out of Paris and the density of traffic was a little unnerving even for a licensed driver. With our little Wanderer machine we constantly had cars, lorries and also bigger motorcycles buzzing past us on our left, often so close that on two occasions I really feared being driven off the road.

I began to wonder whether we had made the right decision in choosing this route to Paris. We stopped in a roadside parking and rest area to consult our map again for an alternative route. However, we quickly came to the conclusion that with the existing time constraint the current highway was undoubtedly the quickest way of completing this day's journey and we simply had to accept the driving hazards. Gert said rather laconically that on those two occasions we were probably targeted by some Frenchmen with long painful memories who had noticed the 'D' on our back numberplate. If that were true I am glad to say that it never happened again for the rest of our journey through France.

After by-passing Evreux, traffic became even heavier but thankfully also slower and we began to feel confident that we would reach Paris in good time.

The remaining question was: where in that large metropolis was the university?

We reached the Paris outskirts early in the afternoon and when Gert spotted a newsagent and stationery shop we stopped to buy a street map of Paris on which we soon found the location of the university campus. It came as a most welcome surprise when we discovered that the well-signposted N13 route would take us almost directly to our final destination. Having experienced fast-moving inner-city traffic before in Strassburg and Metz, I felt quite confident that I could manoeuvre my way through central Paris, but I have to admit that I heaved a great sigh of relief when we finally reached the Avenue de la République and the campus building. A young lady in the bursar's office told Gert that two single rooms had been booked for us for three nights and that the charges would be taken care of by the person who made the booking. There was also a secure bicycle shed where we could park our motorcycle. It all sounded too good to be true.

The room, as to be expected, was a sparsely furnished student quarter but with a comfortable-looking bed. After having slept on a thin quilted groundsheet every night so far, this bed looked a real luxury. An equally treasured luxury was the bath- and shower-room at the end of the corridor. With constantly having been on the road and with our overnight camping, we were both beginning to have a slight personal hygiene problem.

After a quick clean-up we hurried back to the bursar's office where Gert phoned his cousin to confirm our arrival and to agree on a meeting point for the following day. Meanwhile I tried my limited French on that pretty young office lady to see if she could provide me with a map of the Paris Metro system, because it had become abundantly clear to me that I was not going to use our motorcycle for any sightseeing during our stay here. The young lady not only presented me with a Metro map but gave me a host of leaflets with historic data about Paris, the university and some of the landmark buildings in this fascinating metropolis.

Although tiring, all in all we considered it to have been a very successful day and to crown it all we decided to treat ourselves in a nearby restaurant to a proper meal and a couple of glasses of wine. The prospect of spending the night in a comfortable bed added to a general feeling of contentment.

What a pity we would only be here only for two days.

The next morning, refreshed and with me having put on my last remaining clean shirt, we studied the Paris road map and the Metro plan to see how best to reach the agreed meeting place with Gert's cousin. Apart from agreeing the meeting time, the rest of the arrangement had been left rather vague and all Gert could tell me was that we would be meeting his cousin in the first large café on the right-hand side at the very bottom of the Champs Elysées, just off the Place de la Concorde.

Years back, during our time in Berlin, I had my first experience with underground transport systems and therefore the Paris Metro was not such a novelty to me as it was to Gert, who had never seen or used an underground rail system before. He looked quite bewildered when we descended into the first Metro station but soon seemed to enjoy the speed at which we were reaching station after station. When we ascended finally at the Place de la Concorde he said: "I am glad we left our little Wanderer in the bicycle shed."

The café was easily identifiable and as we approached it, Gert started waving at a young lady sitting alone at a table just outside the main entrance. When she rose from her table I was quite astonished how tall she was, but I was also glad I had made myself as presentable as possible because this young lady was a picture of Parisian elegance. Gert told me later that his cousin had come to Paris two years ago and was working on the publishing side of a French fashion magazine.

The two cousins brought themselves up-to-date on family matters and thereafter over a delicious coffee and pastry cousin Denise gave us a number of suggestions on what to visit during our short stay. Gert and I had already decided that we could not return to Freiburg without being able to tell friends and family that we had at least climbed the Eiffel Tower, even if it was only up to the first platform.

Denise suggested giving the Palace and the Gardens of Versailles a miss because it would take up a full day of our short visit and should be reserved for a return in the future.

"Go up to Montmartre," she said. "Enjoy the bohemian atmosphere of the artistic quarters and visit some of the early Parisian markets which give you a real flavour of this vibrant city."

All too soon Denise had to excuse herself as she had to return to her office and we both thanked her not only for having arranged our accommodation but also for having so generously paid for it.

And you two scroungers, so it seems, did not even think of bringing her some flowers or a little gift.

You are absolutely right. It was an unforgivable faux pas and we both felt rather ashamed of our lack of etiquette.

Following Denise's advice we criss-crossed Paris on foot and by Metro, climbed up the Eiffel Tower in sweltering heat, and even went for a short cruise on the Seine. Thankfully the campus compound remained open until midnight, which allowed us to savour the late-evening atmosphere of the bohemian quarters.

The moment of our departure came all too soon. The charming young lady in the office told me that the bicycle shed would be accessible from seven o'clock in the morning which would allow us to make an early start for our journey back towards Freiburg. Gert and I had already agreed that on this stretch we would travel via Nancy and from there over the Vosges mountains to Colmar, finally crossing the Rhine at Breisach. A rough calculation gave us a distance of just under 500 kilometres, which meant one more night camping. After the comfort of the Paris campus quarters, camping had lost some of its old appeal.

The early morning traffic was fast and noisy and I was very relieved when after some hazardous driving we finally reached the quieter eastern outskirts of Paris. Our next target was Epernay and beyond that a place called St Dizier. By then, we thought we would have made the halfway mark to Freiburg and would start looking for a suitable camping site. With quite a lot of open countryside ahead of us, Gert wanted to have another go at driving our motorcycle, to which I willingly agreed because his competence and confidence had risen so much that the only remaining fear was a police patrol car flagging us down with Gert at the handlebars and him not being able to produce a driving licence. I told him that with all the tuition I had given him he should get his own licence with the greatest of ease once back in Freiburg.

After a short stop for petrol and provisions at St Dizier we continued our journey towards Nancy. With Nancy still a few kilometres away the road crossed a very picturesque valley, with a road sign telling us that we were travelling alongside the Marne canal. The meadows along the embankment looked ideal for us to make this our last night of camping and so we did. As this was our last night we treated ourselves to a festive dinner with bread, cheese and sausages and even a bottle of wine, all of which resulted in a good night's sleep. In the morning Gert folded up our little tent for the last time and we set off on the last leg of our journey.

We decided to bypass Nancy and to head straight for the Vosges hills. I had read somewhere that some of the roads over the mountains were very steep. Our motorcycle, after all, had only a 125cc engine and we realised we may be forced to dismount on some stretches and push the motorcycle uphill ourselves. Gert, now an enthusiastic motorcyclist, dismissed my concerns and told me to have more faith in our remarkably reliable little engine. And he was right. The road was steep in parts, but our Wanderer motorcycle took us up to the top without displaying any signs of strain or overheating and we soon started our long descend down to Colmar. Being back in Alsace, my thoughts went back again to my days as a child evacuee in Broock and Louis, the French prisoner of war who had been such a kind and caring friend to me. If by chance he had walked along here in Colmar, would I still have recognised him? After all, nearly fifteen years had passed since then.

The border post at the Rhine bridge was quite busy with a number of French cars heading for Germany. Gert told me that the tyre- and motor-accessories traders in Freiburg did a good business with French motorists because prices in Germany were considerably lower. It sounded a reasonable explanation for the long queue we had to join at the French border post. As we moved up the line I recognised some of the buildings from my more turbulent days as a member of the European Youth Movement, when at this border post we had demonstrated with our French counterparts for a new vision for our continent.

On the Breisach side of the river the border control was swift and with the familiar contours of the Kaiserstuhl on our left we made quick progress towards Freiburg. Gert mentioned again that one of his first actions would be to book himself in for a driving test for motorcycles.

Once back in Freiburg we first drove to the camping store to return our slightly damaged tent. The shop owner reminded us that at the time of hire he had suggested we take out an insurance but that we had declined. He took a closer look at the damage and conceded that for five Marks the hole could be patched over. Gert then unrolled our quilted groundsheet and the shop owner was only too happy to accept this in lieu of the previously stated five Marks.

Thereafter we returned our Wanderer motorcycle to the leasing company, expressing our great satisfaction with the remarkable performance of this machine. We did not think that the company owner would have liked to hear that his remarkable little machine had performed also very well when driven by a non-licence holder.

To finish off the holiday properly we had a leisurely drink at the Münster Platz before returning to our respective homes.

Presumably you were looking forward to a more settled period now, with time on your hands to involve yourself again in the political arena and no doubt also wondering about your career progression.

Yes, Joseph, you are absolutely right. These were, in fact, topics we both discussed over our drink at the Münster Platz. Gert worked for a company which developed and manufactured medical appliances and he was very positive about good career opportunities in the years to come.

Having already enjoyed a good career progression, I also had good reason to have healthy expectation for the future - but I had also noticed that in the commercial departments some of the senior clerks and correspondents had been there for many years, with few openings for further advancement or career changes. However I need not have worried about all this, as other events occurred to shape my future life.

It must have been just before my birthday in February when, before settling down in my office, the department manager asked me to go to the company boardroom. I had never seen this room before with its beautiful long polished table and ornate chairs round it. Apart from Dr Mez, our managing director, our sales director and the Scottish departmental manager, there was also another gentleman sitting at the end of the table, who - judging by his apparel - was not a Freiburg resident. On entering the room I had already noticed that the gentlemen were conversing in English. Dr Mez then explained to me in German that our visitor was Lord Glentana from Scotland and that he had come to our company in Freiburg to see if we could provide a candidate for a management apprenticeship with the mother company of Mez AG, the Coats Group in Glasgow. The Freiburg management had considered me to be a possible candidate, which was the reason I was now being presented to our visitor.

At this stage the visitor rose from his chair, displaying in full his elegant pin-striped suit, and started to ask me questions. My rudimentary knowledge of the English language was completely insufficient to understand any of the questions and the whole exchange had to be done with the linguistic assistance of Dr Mez and the Scottish departmental manager.

The whole interview lasted less than half an hour, during the course of which I was asked about my family background, how and where my father served during the war, if I had lost any family members during the war, what I had done after 1945, whether I spoke any foreign languages plus a lot of questions about my personal hobbies. One additional question was whether I had a valid passport. All this questioning, although being very intrusive, took place in a relaxed and friendly atmosphere, which helped very much to overcome my initial nervousness.

With a friendly 'goodbye' from the visitor, I was finally dismissed. Back in my office my manager and colleagues were all extremely curious as to why I had been called to the boardroom, but on the instructions of Dr Mez I refrained from giving any information.

When I got home from work that evening I had a lot to report and thankfully my parents looked upon it very positively and as a great opportunity for me, should I succeed in being chosen.

The next day Dr Mez called me into his office again to inform me that the interview had been successful and that if I agreed, arrangement would be made for me to travel to Glasgow at the beginning of April for a Management Training Course of at least two years. I gave my agreement there and then, but drew his attention to the fact that I would have very serious communication problems due to my very limited knowledge of the English language. He dismissed this as being only a minor obstacle and assured me that the people in Glasgow would render all the necessary assistance.

"With your approval now," he said, "the company will deal with all the administrative aspects of visa and work-permit application and the railway ticket to Glasgow."

After all the railway journeys in post-war East Germany, this was going to be my longest journey yet and hopefully also the least hazardous. Then there was the added bonus that I would be spending a night in London, not in a station waiting-room but in a proper hotel, details of which I would be receiving with my travel documents. I was also informed that one of our sales representatives will shortly join me in the office to take over my present responsibilities.

During this brief face-to-face encounter with Dr Mez I gained the impression that he was quite pleased, if not proud, that the Scottish parent company had chosen a trainee candidate from his subsidiary company here in Freiburg. Finally he informed me that on my arrival at Glasgow central station I was to carry a German newspaper under my arm to identify me to the person sent to collect me.

Many evenings of the following weeks were filled with farewell parties with school and college friends, a visit to my now widowed grandfather and to a variety of people who had become part of our social circle. I even attended an evening meeting of my old fellow members of the European Youth Movement, whose passion and enthusiasm did not seem to have waned from the early days of its inception.

During these days I became aware how much I had become part again of the town I now called my home. Gert could hardly believe it when I told him about my new venture.

"When we were in Deauville recently and you stared out onto the sea," he said, "I did not realise that so soon afterwards you would want to cross it."

The great day finally arrived. My mother, probably like most mothers, suggested that she should pack my suitcase for me and on this special occasion I did not put up any opposition.

It was a rather grey April afternoon when we left our home for the railway station. My brothers Lothar and Dietmar had said their goodbyes the evening before and now my parents accompanied me to the railway station. In the station I remembered that on arrival in Glasgow I was supposed to carry a German newspaper under my arm. I bought the *Frankfurter Allgemeine* there and then because I did not expect newsagents in Calais or London to sell such papers.

The parting on the platform was less emotional than I had expected. I even found an empty compartment, which augured well for an overnight trip that strangely enough would take me through Metz, the place with happy memories from my recent holiday with Gert.

When wishing me a final farewell, my parents looked very composed and I was beginning to wonder whether they had fully realised that this was not just a short holiday but a long period of absence. Maybe parting had become an accepted feature in our family life, with our year-long separation from our father and my own frequent journeys into the unknown in my childhood and teenage days. It seems it was something we had learned to accept and live with.

And yet, as I leant out of the window to wave my final goodbye, all sorts of thoughts flooded through my mind. Was this allegedly career-advancing adventure really worth giving up family life, friends and colleagues for such a long period? And Freiburg itself, the town that had brought our family together again and which I now regarded as my home town.

However, here I was and there was no going back as the train was gathering speed out of Freiburg station, heading north.

After settling down to read the newspaper I got out my English Phrasebook for Travellers to prepare myself a little bit more for the linguistic challenges I would face on the other side of the Channel. I also tried to familiarise myself with the strange English currency with divisions of twelfths and twentieths, which looked so complicated compared with the metric system of Continental currencies.

Finally, after some hours of sleep, I awoke to find the train pulling into Calais. It was 23 April 1957 and another border crossing with life-changing consequences was about to take place.

Well, Joseph, here we come to the end of a 23-year time span which I hope has given you an insight into how an infant developed into adulthood during one of the most horrific periods in modern European history. Thank you for being such a patient listener and also for your searching questions. However tumultuous and unorthodox my passage through those years may have been, it left me with a strong impression that even after such bloody confrontations there is a conciliatory streak left in us human beings, which I hope bodes well for my future journey.

Thank you, Wolfgang, for letting me share your reminiscences with you. Having coped with the ups and downs over the last 23 years, I suggest that you are now adequately equipped to cope with any challenges in the years ahead. I wish you well on your journey and maybe in a few years' time another opportunity will arise to share another bottle of Alsace Riesling with you.

TRICORN
BOOKS

www.tricornbooks.co.uk